Ideas to stretch food budgets

This special edition of "Most for the Money Main Dishes" is designed for today's cook. It presents recipes and ideas that save food budgets yet deliver real value, many of which feature PREMIUM Saltine Crackers by Nabisco and CAMPBELL'S Soups.

In the constant stretch-the-budget game, flexibility is a big plus. Be ever alert to seasonal specials, sales and coupon redemptions and ready to substitute ingredients—but remember the lowest price is not always the best buy.

Always look for quality and reliability in ingredients. The foods you prepare, however inexpensive, should always be appealing and delicious. This cookbook with its tempting main dishes, quick soup and salad combinations, practical tips on freezing foods and using leftovers is really a gold mine of good information.

We hope you use it often and have the fun of eating deliciously on a slim budget.

Claire Boasi *Margaret Happel*

Claire Boasi
Director of Home Economics
Campbell Soup Company

Margaret Happel
Director of Consumer Affairs
Nabisco, Inc.

WILTED LETTUCE SALAD

6 cups shredded iceberg
  lettuce
¼ cup sliced scallions
¼ cup sliced radishes
8 ounces sliced bologna,
  cut in strips

6 bacon slices, diced
¼ cup wine vinegar
½ teaspoon seasoned salt
2 hard-cooked eggs,
  chopped
Saltine crackers

In large salad bowl, combine lettuce, scallions, radishes and bologna. In medium skillet, fry bacon over medium heat until crisp. Remove bacon with slotted spoon; add to salad bowl. Add vinegar and salt to skillet. Bring to a boil, stirring. Pour over salad; toss. Garnish with eggs. Serve with Cheddar Corn Chowder and saltine crackers. Makes 4 main-dish servings.

CHEDDAR CORN CHOWDER

2 cans (11 ounces each)
  condensed Cheddar
  cheese soup
1 soup can water
1 soup can milk

1 can (8 ounces) corn,
  drained
¼ cup finely chopped
  green pepper
Liquid hot pepper
  seasoning
Saltine crackers

In large saucepan, combine soup, water, milk, corn and green pepper. Cover and simmer 5 minutes. Add liquid hot pepper seasoning to taste. Serve with Wilted Lettuce Salad and saltine crackers. Serves 4.

DRESSING WELL: A well-seasoned dressing is essential for any salad. Basic know-how: oil and vinegar dressings are best when made with twice as much oil as vinegar. Both the oil and vinegar—as well as the seasonings—give character to the dressing. Olive oil is more pungent and noticeable; peanut, corn or safflower oils are lighter. Vinegar adds sharpness—red wine vinegar is the most intense; apple cider is the mildest. And lemon juice is a delicate substitute for either.

ORIENTAL SPINACH SALAD

5 cups fresh spinach, washed and torn into bite-size pieces
2 cans (5 ounces each) chunk white chicken
1 can (16 ounces) bean sprouts, drained
1 can (8 ounces) water chestnuts, drained and sliced
1 jar (4 ounces) sliced pimientos, drained
1 small green pepper, cut in strips
2 tablespoons toasted sesame seeds
½ cup vegetable oil
¼ cup cider vinegar
1 tablespoon soy sauce
1 garlic clove, crushed
Saltine crackers

In large bowl, combine spinach, chicken, bean sprouts, water chestnuts, pimientos, green pepper and sesame seeds. In covered jar or small bowl, blend together oil, vinegar, soy sauce and garlic; pour over salad. Toss to blend. Serve with Chinese Chicken Broth and saltine crackers. Makes 4 main-dish servings.

CHINESE CHICKEN BROTH

2 cans (10¾ ounces each) condensed chicken broth
2 soup cans water
½ teaspoon garlic powder
½ teaspoon ground ginger
½ cup sliced radishes
2 tablespoons sliced scallions
Saltine crackers

In large saucepan, combine chicken broth, water, garlic powder and ginger. Cover and simmer 5 minutes. Add radishes and scallions before serving. Serve with Oriental Spinach Salad and saltine crackers. Serves 4.

TURKEY CHEF SALAD

6 cups mixed greens
6 ounces Swiss cheese, cut
  in strips (1½ cups)
1 can (5 ounces) chunk
  turkey
1 cup cauliflowerettes
1 cup thinly sliced zucchini
1 cup halved cherry
  tomatoes
⅔ cup bottled herb & spice
  dressing
Saltine crackers

In large salad bowl, combine greens, cheese, turkey, cauliflowerettes, zucchini and tomatoes. Pour dressing over salad; toss. Serve with Curried Asparagus Soup and saltine crackers. Makes 6 main-dish servings.

CURRIED ASPARAGUS SOUP

2 cans (10¾ ounces each)
  condensed cream of
  asparagus soup
2 soup cans milk
¾ teaspoon curry powder
1 jar (2 ounces)
  diced pimientos, drained
Yogurt or sour cream
Saltine crackers

Empty soup into large bowl. Slowly blend in milk; stir in curry powder and pimientos. Chill 2 hours or until serving time. Garnish with a dollop of yogurt or sour cream. Serve with Turkey Chef Salad and saltine crackers. Serves 6.

KNOW YOUR VEGGIES: There's more to salads then just tomatoes and lettuce. Young garden vegetables of any and every description can be cut, sliced and grated and added to a salad bowl. Try thinly sliced fresh mushrooms, tiny sprigs of broccoli, young asparagus spears sliced diagonally, Chinese style, and young fresh green beans similarly prepared. Judiciously add paper thin onion rings, red or white radishes, slivers of scallions or hot green chili peppers.

MARINATED GARDEN SALAD

1 can (16 ounces) sliced
    beets, drained
1 small onion, cut in thin
    rings
1 can (20 ounces) white
    kidney beans, drained
1 cucumber, cut in 2-inch
    strips
⅓ cup wine vinegar

⅓ cup vegetable oil
¼ cup chopped parsley
½ teaspoon salt
Lettuce leaves
8 ounces sliced ham, rolled
8 ounces muenster
    cheese, sliced
Saltine crackers

Toss beets and onion. Arrange with beans and cucumber
separately in 2-quart oblong baking dish. In measuring
cup, blend vinegar, oil, parsley and salt; pour over vegetables. Cover and chill at least 2 hours. Arrange lettuce on
serving platter. Mound beans in center and surround, in
sections, with beets, cucumber, ham and cheese. Serve
with Continental Mushroom Soup and saltine crackers.
Makes 6 main-dish servings.

CONTINENTAL MUSHROOM SOUP

2 cans (10¾ ounces each)
    condensed golden mush-
    room soup
2 soup cans water
2 tablespoons sherry or
    lemon juice

2 teaspoons
    Worcestershire sauce
Freeze-dried or frozen
    chopped chives
Saltine crackers

In large saucepan, combine soup, water, sherry or lemon
juice and Worcestershire sauce. Cover and simmer 5 minutes. Ladle into serving bowls. Sprinkle with chopped
chives. Serve with Marinated Garden Salad and saltine
crackers. Serves 6.

MEDITERRANEAN SALAD

Lettuce leaves
8 ounces sliced Genoa
  salami, rolled
3 navel oranges, peeled
  and sliced
8 ounces process sliced
  American cheese, rolled

½ cup whole pitted black
  olives
¼ cup red onion rings
Bottled red wine vinegar
  dressing
Saltine crackers

Line large oval platter with lettuce leaves. Arrange salami, orange slices, cheese and olives in sections on platter. Garnish with onion rings. Serve dressing alongside salad. Serve with Creamy Vegetable Soup and saltine crackers. Makes 6 main-dish servings.

CREAMY VEGETABLE SOUP

2 cans (10½ ounces each)
  condensed vegetable
  soup
2 soup cans milk
½ teaspoon basil leaves

Liquid hot pepper
  seasoning
Imitation bacon bits
Saltine crackers

Combine soup and 1 soup can milk in blender. Blend on low speed until smooth. Pour into large saucepan. Add remaining milk, basil and liquid hot pepper seasoning to taste. Cover and simmer 5 minutes. Ladle into serving bowls. Garnish with bacon bits. Serve with Mediterranean Salad and saltine crackers. Serves 6.

THE ZIP AND ZEST OF SALADS: Refreshing salads have an extra fillip from very special ingredients. Olives, whether black or green, pimiento-stuffed or packed in brine, add an exciting flavor note. So does crumbled blue cheese, or a sprinkling of capers, or finely chopped anchovies. As a last minute topping, use crisp, crumbled, bacon or garlicky croutons.

HAM 'N CHEESE COLE SLAW

¾ cup mayonnaise
2 tablespoons cider vinegar
1 teaspoon salt
1 teaspoon celery seed
¼ teaspoon pepper
6 cups coarsely shredded
   cabbage

1½ cups diced cooked
   ham (about 10 ounces)
1 cup sliced celery
1 medium green pepper,
   cut in strips
8 ounces process
   American cheese, cut in
   strips
Saltine crackers

In large bowl, blend together mayonnaise, vinegar, salt, celery seed and pepper. Add cabbage, ham, celery and green pepper; toss to blend. Chill 1 hour or until serving time. Arrange cheese around edge of bowl. Serve with Garden Pea Soup and saltine crackers. Makes 6 main-dish servings.

GARDEN PEA SOUP

2 tablespoons butter or
   margarine
1 cup coarsely grated
   carrot
⅓ cup chopped onion
2 cans (11¼ ounces each)
   condensed green pea
   soup

2 soup cans water
2 teaspoons prepared
   mustard
Saltine crackers

In large saucepan, heat butter or margarine; sauté carrot and onion 2 minutes. Add soup, water and mustard. Cover and simmer 5 minutes. Serve with Ham 'n Cheese Cole Slaw and saltine crackers. Serves 6.

TUNA GAZPACHO SALAD

Lettuce leaves
2 cans (7 ounces each)
 tuna, drained and
 chunked
1 large cucumber,
 coarsely chopped
2 medium green peppers,
 coarsely chopped

2 medium tomatoes, cut
 into wedges
⅓ cup vegetable oil
¼ cup tomato juice
¼ cup wine vinegar
1 teaspoon garlic salt
Dash liquid hot pepper
 seasoning
Saltine crackers

Place lettuce leaves on serving platter; arrange tuna, cucumber and green peppers in sections; surround platter with tomato wedges. In covered jar or small bowl, blend together oil, tomato juice, vinegar, garlic salt and liquid hot pepper seasoning; serve alongside salad with Cheesy Onion Soup and saltine crackers. Makes 6 main-dish servings.

CHEESY ONION SOUP

2 cans (10½ ounces each)
 condensed onion soup
2 soup cans water

¼ cup chopped parsley
6 ounces Swiss cheese,
 grated (about 1½ cups)
Saltine crackers

In large saucepan, combine soup, water and parsley. Cover and simmer 5 minutes. Divide cheese among 6 serving bowls; ladle in soup. Serve with Tuna Gazpacho Salad and saltine crackers. Serves 6.

SALAD LORE: The best salads are cool and crisp and this means keeping all salad makings in the refrigerator—even canned meats, fish and salad dressing ingredients. In the interests of freshness—and nutrition—tear lettuce and cut salad vegetables at the last minute. Cut vegetables which are stored quickly loose their crunch and nutritional value. Looking for an alternate to cucumber? Try young zucchini with its tender green skin and buttery-white flesh.

A *Campbell* COOKBOOK

MOST-FOR-THE-MONEY

main
dishes

Recipes Developed and Tested by
Home Economists of Campbell Kitchens

Photographer · G. William Holland

introduction

Most-for-the-money main dishes . . . tasty, satisfying, easily prepared. Dishes that are kind to your pocketbook. That's exactly what you'll find between these covers. The recipes call for on-hand ingredients and include canned Condensed Soups and Chunky Soups—those hard-working pantry staples which help make a little go a long way, deliciously.

Whether you use Campbell's Soups as an appetizer, a quick sauce, or an integral part of casseroles and stove-top dishes, they pay handsome dividends in time, energy, and quality.

And quality, flavor, and nutrition are important. The recipes in this book show how you can serve good food from skillet, oven, or saucepan—meal after imaginative meal. All this without breaking the bank.

Some of the recipes are meatless; some are designed for a crowd. There's even a section featuring everything *but* main dishes!

Whatever you choose to make, two things are certain: You'll enjoy serving the best for less, and everyone else will simply enjoy. Happy eating!

table of contents

a primer on nutrition

Nutrition on a budget? You bet! It's one area where your knowledge counts more than what's in your wallet. Once you know which foods and how much of each your family needs every day, the choices are yours. Even the most expensive food item has a less costly cousin to provide needed nutrients. Broiled lobster may be your first love, yet an equal amount of canned tuna supplies the same high quality protein for dollars less—and it can be equally as tempting.

Here is a practical guide to good nutrition: The Four Food Groups.

VEGETABLE AND FRUIT GROUP — 4 or more servings

MILK GROUP — 2 or more servings

MEAT GROUP — 2 or more servings

BREAD AND CEREAL GROUP — 4 or more servings

Simply keep track of the number of servings required from each group every day and plan your menus accordingly. Be sure to include everything—snacks and food eaten away from home, too.

Because foods from the Meat Group eat up the greatest part of your grocery dollar—and are the most important protein source—they almost always are featured in the main dish. So what better place to start a menu plan? Think of the entrée as the hub of the meal and let foods from the other groups—fruits, vegetables, breads, dairy products, "extras" . . . revolve around it.

Here are several menus. Use them as is or adjust them to fit your family's preferences, nutritional needs, and eating patterns.

"V-8" Cocktail Vegetable Juice
Stuffed Flounder Roll-ups
(page 61)
Fluffy Buttered Rice
Pepper Slaw
Baking-Powder Biscuits
Chocolate Cake
Coffee - Tea - Milk

Jumbo Tuna Gumbo
(page 99)
Hearts of Lettuce
with
Green Goddess Dressing
Hard Rolls
Cheesecake Pie
(page 110)

Oven Fried Chicken
Scalloped Potatoes
(page 104)
Molded Carrot &
Pineapple Salad
Brownie
Coffee - Tea - Milk

Tamale Pie
(page 11)
Tossed Salad with
Dressing
Mixed Fruit & Melon Cup
Coffee - Tea - Milk

When it comes time to select foods for other menus CONTRAST is the key to success. Balance Tomato-Mushroom Rabbit (page 73) with crisp salad greens. Accent mellow Chicken Zucchini Skillet (page 54) with tangy cranberry relish. Couple the vibrant colors of broccoli or tomatoes with the muted tones of Easy Oven Fillets (page 75).

In other words, make meals appetizing to the last forkful. Empty plates mean nutrients-at-work and money well-spent.

Here again, the budget takes a back seat to brainwork. With thoughtful planning and careful preparation, anyone can put together a million dollar meal at five and dime prices. The simplest, pennywise dishes are memorable when done to perfection and served with flair.

# of casseroles and compliments

Nothing compares to the mingling of hearty flavors in a piping hot casserole. So smile as you tuck one of the following dishes neatly into the oven. Your family will when they catch a whiff of that *"come and get it"* aroma. And again when they dig in. Cheers to the cook!

DEEP DISH TURKEY PIE

1 cup sliced celery
Generous dash onion
  powder
2 tablespoons butter or
  margarine
1 can (10¾ ounces)
  condensed cream of
  chicken soup
1½ cups cubed cooked
  turkey or chicken

1½ cups cooked carrots
  cut in 1-inch pieces
¼ cup milk
2 teaspoons lemon juice
⅛ teaspoon ground
  nutmeg
½ cup biscuit mix
2 tablespoons cold water

In saucepan, cook celery with onion in butter until tender. Stir in remaining ingredients except biscuit mix and water. Bring to boil; stir occasionally. Meanwhile, to make pastry, combine biscuit mix and water. Roll pastry to fit top of 1-quart casserole. Pour hot chicken mixture into casserole; top with pastry. Trim edges; make several slits in pastry. Bake at 450°F. for 15 minutes or until done. Makes about 3½ cups.

TUNA VERDÉ

2 packages (10 ounces
  each) frozen chopped
  spinach, cooked and
  drained
1 can (11 ounces)
  condensed Cheddar
  cheese soup
1 can (about 7 ounces)
  tuna, drained and flaked

2 hard-cooked eggs,
  chopped
½ cup chopped canned
  tomatoes
⅛ teaspoon oregano
  leaves, crushed
2 tablespoons buttered
  bread crumbs

Combine all ingredients except bread crumbs. Pour into 1½-quart shallow baking dish (10x6x2"). Bake at 450°F. for 20 minutes or until hot; stir. Top with crumbs; bake 5 minutes more. Makes about 4 cups.

FIRST THINGS FIRST: You can prevent staples and canned goods from becoming has-beens by rotating them so that the oldest is always used first. Better yet, date packages at time of purchase.

BEST EVER MEAT LOAF

1 can (10¾ ounces)
  condensed cream of
  mushroom or golden
  mushroom soup
2 pounds ground beef
½ cup fine dry bread
  crumbs

⅓ cup finely chopped
  onion
1 egg, slightly beaten
1 teaspoon salt
⅓ cup water

Mix *thoroughly* ½ cup soup, beef, bread crumbs, onion, egg, and salt. Shape *firmly* into loaf (8x4″); place in shallow baking pan. Bake at 375°F. for 1 hour 15 minutes. Blend remaining soup, water, and 2 to 3 tablespoons drippings. Heat; stir occasionally. Serve with loaf. Makes 6 servings.

Frosted Meat Loaf: Prepare loaf as above; bake for 1 hour. Frost loaf with 4 cups mashed potatoes; sprinkle with shredded Cheddar cheese. Bake 15 minutes more. Serve with sauce.

Swedish Meat Loaf: Add ½ teaspoon nutmeg to loaf. Blend remaining soup with ⅓ cup sour cream; omit drippings and water. Serve over loaf; sprinkle with additional nutmeg. Garnish with thinly sliced cucumber.

Meat Loaf Wellington:
Crescent Rolls (Refrigerated): Prepare loaf as above. Bake at 375°F. for 1 hour. Spoon off fat. Separate 1 package (8 ounces) refrigerated crescent dinner rolls; place crosswise over top and down sides of meat loaf, overlapping slightly. Bake 15 minutes more. Serve with sauce.
Patty Shells: Thaw 1 package (10 ounces) frozen puff pastry patty shells. Prepare loaf as above. Bake at 375°F. for 30 minutes. Spoon off fat. Increase oven temperature to 400°F. On floured board, roll 5 patty shells into rectangle (12x8″); prick several times with fork. Cover top and sides of loaf with pastry. Decorate top with remaining patty shell, rolled and cut into fancy shapes. Bake for 45 minutes more or until golden brown. Serve with sauce.

UPSIDE-DOWN MEAT PIE

1 pound ground beef
½ cup chopped celery
½ cup chopped onion
¼ cup chopped green
  pepper
1 can (10¾ ounces)
  condensed tomato soup

1 teaspoon prepared
  mustard
1½ cups biscuit mix
⅓ cup cold water
3 slices (about 3 ounces)
  process cheese, cut in
  half diagonally

In 10″ oven-proof skillet, brown beef and cook celery, onion, and green pepper until tender (use shortening if necessary). Stir to separate meat; *drain well*. Stir in soup and mustard. Combine biscuit mix and water; roll or pat dough into a circle slightly smaller than skillet. Spread meat mixture evenly in skillet; top with biscuit dough. Bake at 450°F. for 15 minutes or until browned. Turn upside down on platter. Top with cheese. Cut in wedges and serve. Makes 6 servings.

BAKED CHICKEN WITH NOODLES

2 pounds chicken parts
1 tablespoon melted
  butter or margarine
1 can (10¾ ounces)
  condensed chicken
  broth
½ cup water

2 teaspoons Italian salad
  dressing mix
1 teaspoon sesame seed
3 cups uncooked medium
  noodles
1 package (9 ounces)
  frozen cut green beans
Paprika

In 2-quart shallow baking dish (12x8x2″), arrange chicken skin-side down. Pour butter over. Bake at 400°F. for 20 minutes; remove chicken. Stir in remaining ingredients except paprika. Arrange chicken skin-side up on noodle mixture; sprinkle with paprika. Bake covered 40 minutes more or until done. Stir noodle mixture before serving. Makes 4 servings.

OUT OF THE APPLE BARREL . . . *into the refrigerator. Apples are less likely to deteriorate when stored in the refrigerator. Following harvest in the fall they may be kept in any cool place (below 60°F.).*

BURGER-RICE BAKE

2 cans (19 ounces each)
  chunky sirloin burger
  soup
1 cup quick-cooking rice,
  uncooked

1 cup stewed tomatoes
2 teaspoons chili powder

In 1½-quart shallow baking dish (10x6x2"), combine ingredients. Bake at 400°F. for 25 minutes or until rice is done; stir. Garnish with sliced hard-cooked egg if desired. Makes about 5 cups.

KNOCKWURST AND CABBAGE

1 small head cabbage
  (about 1 pound), cut in 4
  wedges
1 can (10¾ ounces)
  condensed cream of
  celery soup

¼ cup milk
1 cup chopped apple
½ teaspoon caraway seed
1 pound knockwurst
  (4 links), slashed

In saucepan, cook cabbage in boiling water 10 minutes; drain. In 1½-quart shallow baking dish (10x6x2"), arrange cabbage. Combine soup, milk, apple, and caraway; pour over cabbage. Arrange knockwurst between cabbage wedges. Bake at 400°F. for 25 minutes or until hot. Stir sauce before serving. Makes 4 servings.

WAGONWHEEL TUNA BAKE

1 can (10¾ ounces)
  condensed cream of
  mushroom soup
2 cups cooked rice
⅓ cup milk
1 tablespoon lemon juice

2 cans (about 7 ounces
  each) tuna, drained and
  flaked
1 package (10 ounces)
  frozen broccoli spears,
  cooked and drained
½ cup shredded process
  cheese

In 9" round baking dish, combine soup, rice, milk, lemon, and tuna. Bake at 400°F. for 20 minutes; stir. Arrange broccoli in spoke-fashion on top of rice mixture; sprinkle with cheese. Bake 10 minutes more or until hot. Makes 4 servings.

TAMALE PIE

1 pound ground beef
½ cup chopped onion
⅓ cup chopped green
    pepper
1 tablespoon salad oil
1 can (11¼ ounces)
    condensed chili beef
    soup
1 can (16 ounces)
    tomatoes, chopped
⅓ cup sliced ripe olives
2 tablespoons chili powder
1 large clove garlic,
    minced
3 cups water
1 cup corn meal

½ teaspoon salt
1 cup shredded Cheddar
    cheese

In skillet, brown beef and cook onion and green pepper in oil until tender. Stir to separate meat; pour off fat. Stir in soup, tomatoes, olives, chili powder, and garlic. Cook over low heat 15 minutes; stir occasionally. Meanwhile, bring 2 cups water to boil. Mix corn meal with salt and 1 cup cold water; pour into boiling water, stirring constantly. Cook over medium heat until thickened (about 15 minutes); stir occasionally. Line bottom and sides of buttered 2-quart shallow baking dish (12x8x2″) with cooked corn meal. Fill with chili mixture; bake at 350°F. for 30 minutes. Top with cheese; bake until cheese melts. Makes 6 servings.

PIZZA STRATA

10 slices white bread, cut
    in 1-inch cubes (about 7
    cups)
2 cups shredded sharp
    Cheddar cheese

1 can (10¾ ounces)
    condensed tomato soup
1 soup can water
4 eggs, slightly beaten
1 teaspoon oregano
    leaves, crushed

In buttered 2-quart shallow baking dish (12x8x2″), arrange bread cubes; top with cheese. In bowl, combine remaining ingredients; pour over bread. Cover; refrigerate overnight. Uncover; bake at 350°F. for 30 minutes or until set. Makes 6 servings.

ONE POTATO, TWO POTATO: *Pound for pound, all-purpose potatoes are usually less expensive than baking potatoes. Use them for everything—including baking.*

MEAT 'n' VEGETABLE BAKE

1 can (10¾ ounces)
   condensed cream of
   celery soup
⅓ cup milk
2 tablespoons chopped
   parsley
1 tablespoon pickle relish
½ teaspoon prepared
   mustard
1 can (12 ounces)
   luncheon meat, cubed

1 package (10 ounces)
   frozen cauliflower,
   cooked and drained
1 package (10 ounces)
   frozen mixed
   vegetables, cooked
   and drained
¼ cup buttered bread
   crumbs

In 1½-quart casserole combine all ingredients except bread crumbs. Bake at 350°F. for 25 minutes or until hot; stir. Sprinkle with bread crumbs. Bake 5 minutes more. Makes about 5 cups.

CHILI FRANK ROUNDUP

½ pound frankfurters, cut
   in 1-inch pieces
1 cup chopped onion
2 tablespoons butter or
   margarine
1 can (11¼ ounces)
   condensed chili beef
   soup
½ cup water
¼ cup prepared barbecue
   sauce

1 can (about 8 ounces)
   whole kernel corn,
   drained
2 cups cooked elbow
   macaroni
2 slices (about 2 ounces)
   process cheese, cut in 8
   strips

In saucepan, brown frankfurters and cook onion in butter until tender. Stir in remaining ingredients except cheese. Pour into 1½-quart casserole. Bake at 400°F. for 25 minutes or until hot; stir. Arrange cheese in lattice shape on top of casserole. Bake until cheese melts. Makes about 5½ cups.

TACO CHICKEN

1 can (10¾ ounces)
  condensed cream of
  chicken soup
⅓ cup chili sauce
⅓ cup water
¼ teaspoon hot pepper
  sauce
3 whole chicken breasts
  (about 2 pounds), split

⅓ cup flour
3 cups finely crushed
  taco-flavored corn chips
  (about 10 ounces)
2 tablespoons melted
  butter or margarine

Mix soup, chili sauce, water, and hot pepper sauce. Dust chicken with flour; dip in soup mixture. Roll in chips. Place on rack in shallow baking pan. Drizzle with butter. Bake at 400°F. for 1 hour or until done. Makes 4 servings.

SOUTHWEST FRANKFURTERS

½ cup chopped onion
2 tablespoons butter or
  margarine
1 can (10¾ ounces)
  condensed tomato soup
⅓ cup water
1½ cups cooked spiral-
  shaped macaroni
1 can (about 8 ounces)
  whole kernel golden
  corn, drained

1 tablespoon sweet pickle
  relish
1 teaspoon prepared
  mustard
½ pound frankfurters,
  slashed

In saucepan, cook onion in butter until tender. Stir in remaining ingredients except frankfurters. Pour into 1½-quart shallow baking dish (10x6x2″); top with frankfurters. Bake at 400°F. for 20 minutes or until hot. Makes 4 servings.

IF THE QUALITY FITS, BUY IT: *Grades are one indication of food quality. Lower grades are as nutritious as higher grades, but are often less visually attractive or uniform in size, and should cost less. The end use tells the story.*

CHEESE 'n' NOODLE BAKE

1 can (10¾ ounces)
  condensed cream of
  mushroom soup
¼ cup milk
½ cup drained chopped
  canned tomatoes
¼ teaspoon oregano
  leaves, crushed

Generous dash garlic salt
1½ cups shredded
  process cheese
3 cups cooked large bow
  noodles
Grated Parmesan cheese

In 1½-quart casserole, blend soup, milk, tomatoes, oregano, and garlic salt. Stir in process cheese and noodles. Bake at 400°F. for 25 minutes or until hot; stir. Garnish with Parmesan cheese. Makes about 4½ cups.

HAMBURGER NOODLE STROGANOFF

1 pound ground beef
½ cup chopped onion
1 can (10¾ ounces)
  condensed cream of
  mushroom soup
½ cup sour cream

½ cup water
½ teaspoon paprika
½ teaspoon salt
⅛ teaspoon pepper
2 cups cooked noodles

In skillet, brown beef and cook onion until tender (use shortening if necessary). Stir to separate meat; pour off fat. Add remaining ingredients. Pour into 1½-quart shallow baking dish (10x6x2″). Bake at 400°F. for 25 minutes or until hot; stir. Garnish with tomato slices and buttered bread crumbs the last 5 minutes of baking if desired. Makes about 4½ cups.

CHICKEN PIE AU GRATIN

1 can (19 ounces) chunky
  chicken soup
1 package (10 ounces)
  frozen peas & carrots,
  cooked and drained

1 cup shredded Cheddar
  cheese
⅛ teaspoon rubbed sage
Pastry for 1-crust pie

In 2-quart shallow baking dish (12x8x2″), combine soup, peas & carrots, cheese, and sage. Roll pastry to fit top of dish; place on soup mixture. Trim edges. Sprinkle with paprika if desired. Make several slits in pastry. Bake at 400°F. for 35 minutes or until done. Makes about 3½ cups.

TWO-WAY CASSEROLE

½ cup chopped onion
2 tablespoons butter or
  margarine
1 can (10¾ ounces)
  condensed cream of
  chicken soup
1 can (10¾ ounces)
  condensed cream of
  mushroom soup

⅔ cup milk
½ teaspoon salt
⅛ teaspoon pepper
3 cups cubed cooked
  chicken or ham
4 cups cooked noodles
½ cup shredded Cheddar
  cheese

In saucepan, cook onion in butter until tender; add remaining ingredients except cheese. Pour into 2-quart shallow baking dish (12x8x2″). Bake at 400°F. for 25 minutes or until hot; stir. Top with cheese. Bake until cheese melts. Makes about 7 cups.

PEANUT BUTTER-JELLY STRATA

12 slices white bread
¾ cup chunk-style peanut
  butter
½ cup grape jelly
1 can (10¾ ounces)
  condensed cream of
  chicken soup
1 soup can milk
4 eggs, slightly beaten
Cinnamon
Maple-flavored syrup

Make 6 peanut butter and jelly sandwiches; cut in half diagonally. In 2½-quart shallow baking dish (13x9x2″), arrange sandwich halves overlapping slightly. In bowl, combine soup, milk, and eggs; pour over sandwiches. Sprinkle with cinnamon. Cover; refrigerate 1 hour. Uncover; bake at 350°F. for 30 minutes or until set. Serve with syrup. Makes 6 servings.

HAM AND NOODLE BAKE

1½ cups cubed cooked
  ham or luncheon meat
¼ cup chopped onion
⅛ teaspoon thyme leaves,
  crushed
2 tablespoons butter or
  margarine
1 can (10¾ ounces)
  condensed creamy
  chicken mushroom
  soup

¾ cup water
Generous dash pepper
2 cups cooked noodles
1 cup cooked cut green
  beans
½ cup shredded sharp
  Cheddar cheese

In saucepan, brown ham and cook onion with thyme in butter until tender. Stir in remaining ingredients except cheese. Pour into 1½-quart casserole. Bake at 350°F. for 30 minutes or until hot; stir. Top with cheese; bake until cheese melts. Makes about 5 cups.

HOT DOG! POTATO BAKE

1 can (10¾ ounces)
  condensed cream of
  celery soup
½ cup milk
1 to 2 tablespoons dried
  parsley flakes
1 tablespoon prepared
  mustard

2 cans (about 16 ounces
  each) small whole white
  potatoes, drained and
  sliced
1 pound frankfurters, cut
  in 1-inch pieces

In 2-quart casserole, combine soup, milk, parsley, and mustard; stir in potatoes and frankfurters. Bake at 400°F. for 30 minutes or until hot; stir. Makes about 6 cups.

BAKED MACARONI 'n' CHEESE

1 can (10¾ ounces)
  condensed cream of
  mushroom soup
½ cup milk
½ teaspoon prepared
  mustard

Generous dash pepper
3 cups cooked elbow
  macaroni
2 cups shredded Cheddar
  cheese
1 cup French fried onions

In 1½-quart casserole, blend soup, milk, mustard, and pepper. Stir in macaroni and 1½ cups cheese. Bake at 400°F. for 25 minutes or until hot; stir. Top with onions and remaining cheese; bake 5 minutes more or until cheese melts. Makes about 4½ cups.

THE BIG CHEESE: *When cheese is already grated, shredded, or sliced, you pay extra for handling and packaging. Buy whole pieces and save.*

PORK CHOPS VIA VENETO

6 pork chops (about 1½ pounds)
Salt
Pepper
1 can (10¾ ounces) condensed tomato soup
⅓ cup water
3 cups cooked elbow macaroni
1 cup shredded mild process cheese
⅓ cup finely chopped green pepper
¼ cup finely chopped onion
2 teaspoons Worcestershire
1 teaspoon prepared mustard
Dash hot pepper sauce

In skillet, brown chops (use shortening if necessary); pour off fat. Season with salt and pepper; remove chops from skillet. Add remaining ingredients. Heat until cheese melts. Pour into 2-quart shallow baking dish (12x8x2″); top with chops. Cover; bake at 350°F. for 15 minutes. Uncover; bake 15 minutes more or until done. Makes 4 servings.

PARMESAN CHICKEN

¼ cup fine dry bread crumbs
4 tablespoons grated Parmesan cheese
¼ teaspoon oregano leaves, crushed
Dash garlic powder
Dash pepper
2 pounds chicken parts
1 can (10¾ ounces) condensed cream of mushroom soup
½ cup milk
Paprika

Combine crumbs, 2 tablespoons Parmesan, oregano, garlic, and pepper; roll chicken in mixture. Arrange in 2-quart shallow baking dish (12x8x2″). Bake at 400°F. for 20 minutes. Turn chicken; bake 20 minutes more. Meanwhile, blend soup and milk; pour over chicken. Sprinkle with paprika and remaining Parmesan. Bake 20 minutes more or until done. Arrange chicken on platter. Stir sauce; pour over chicken. Makes 4 servings.

COUNTRY KITCHEN CASSEROLE

1 can (10¾ ounces) condensed cream of mushroom soup
¼ cup water
2 teaspoons prepared mustard
1 teaspoon Worcestershire
1 cup shredded Cheddar cheese

2 cans (about 16 ounces each) small whole white potatoes, drained and sliced
1 package (10 ounces) frozen peas, cooked and drained
1 can (12 ounces) luncheon meat, cut in 6 slices

In bowl, combine soup, water, mustard, Worcestershire, and cheese; add potatoes and peas. Spoon into 1½-quart shallow baking dish (10x6x2″); top with meat. Bake at 400°F. for 25 minutes or until hot. Makes 6 servings.

PORK CHOP 'n' POTATO SCALLOP

4 pork chops (about 1 pound)
Salt
Pepper
1 can (10¾ ounces) condensed cream of mushroom soup

½ cup sour cream
¼ cup water
½ teaspoon dried dill weed, crushed
4 cups thinly sliced potatoes
Parsley

In skillet, brown chops (use shortening if necessary); season with salt and pepper. Blend soup, sour cream, water, and dill. In 2-quart casserole, alternate layers of potatoes and sauce; cover. Bake at 375°F. for 30 minutes. Top with chops. Cover; bake 45 minutes more or until done. Garnish with parsley. Makes 3 servings.

NO-FROST AT LESS COST: *If you have a self-defrosting refrigerator, check the condensate drain every so often to make sure it's clean. A prolonged blockage will cause ice to build up on the coils, making the unit inefficient.*

Clean the condenser coils in the back of the unit, too. In newer refrigerators, the coils are beneath the unit. To clean, remove the front grill and vacuum.

TUNA PUFF

1 can (10¾ ounces)
    condensed cream of
    mushroom soup
½ cup milk
2 cups cooked rice
1 package (10 ounces)
    chopped broccoli,
    cooked and drained
2 cans (about 7 ounces
    each) tuna, drained and
    flaked

⅛ teaspoon ground
    nutmeg
4 eggs, separated
1 tablespoon grated
    Parmesan cheese

In 1½-quart shallow baking dish (10x6x2″), combine soup, milk, rice, broccoli, tuna, and nutmeg. Bake at 400°F. for 20 minutes. Meanwhile, beat egg yolks until thick and lemon-colored; add cheese. Using clean egg beater, beat egg whites until soft peaks form; fold in egg yolk mixture. Remove casserole from oven; stir. Gently spread egg mixture over top. Bake 15 minutes more or until golden brown. Makes about 5 cups.

HAM SPOONBREAD

1 cup finely chopped ham
¼ cup finely chopped
    onion
2 tablespoons butter or
    margarine
1 can (10¾ ounces)
    condensed cream of
    mushroom soup

½ soup can milk
Dash cayenne pepper
½ cup corn meal
3 eggs, separated
Syrup or butter

In saucepan, brown ham and cook onion in butter until tender. Stir in soup, milk, and cayenne. Add corn meal. Bring to boil; reduce heat. Cook until thickened, stirring. Remove from heat. Beat egg yolks until thick and lemon-colored; stir into corn meal mixture. Using clean egg beater, beat egg whites until stiff but not dry. Gradually fold into corn meal mixture. Pour into buttered 1½-quart casserole. Bake at 350°F. for 1 hour. Serve with syrup. Makes 4 servings.

SHEPHERD'S PIE

¼ cup finely chopped
   onion
Generous dash crushed
   thyme leaves
2 tablespoons butter or
   margarine
1 can (10¾ ounces)
   condensed golden
   mushroom soup

¼ cup water
1½ cups cubed cooked
   beef
1 package (10 ounces)
   frozen peas and carrots,
   cooked and drained
4 servings prepared
   instant mashed
   potatoes

In saucepan, cook onion with thyme in butter until tender; add remaining ingredients except potatoes. Pour into 1½-quart casserole. Spoon potatoes around edge of casserole. Bake at 400°F. for 30 minutes or until hot. Makes about 3½ cups.

MEXICALI PIE

1 pound frankfurters, cut
   in 1-inch pieces
1 cup chopped onion
2 tablespoons butter or
   margarine
1 can (10¾ ounces)
   condensed tomato soup
1 can (11¼ ounces)
   condensed chili beef
   soup

1 package (9 ounces)
   frozen cut green beans,
   cooked and drained
¼ cup water
½ package (12 to
   14-ounce size) corn
   muffin mix (about 1 cup)
⅓ cup milk
1 egg

In skillet, brown frankfurters and cook onion in butter until tender. Add soups, beans, and water; bring to boil. Pour into 2-quart shallow baking dish (12x8x2"). Combine corn muffin mix, milk, and egg. Spoon evenly around edge of baking dish. Bake at 400°F. for 20 minutes or until done. Makes about 5½ cups.

BEYOND A LICK AND A PROMISE: *Here's just the incentive you've been needing to clean that oven and broiler: When free of grease and grime, these appliances cook more efficiently, save gas and electricity.*

MEAT-SHELL POTATO PIE

1 can (10¾ ounces)
condensed cream of
mushroom soup
1 pound ground beef
¼ cup finely chopped
onion
1 egg, slightly beaten
¼ cup fine dry bread
crumbs

2 tablespoons chopped
parsley
¼ teaspoon salt
Dash pepper
2 cups mashed potatoes
¼ cup shredded mild
cheese
Cooked bacon, crumbled

Mix *thoroughly* ½ cup soup, beef, onion, egg, bread crumbs, parsley, and seasonings. Press *firmly* into 9-inch pie plate. Bake at 350°F. for 25 minutes; spoon off fat. Frost with potatoes; top with remaining soup, cheese, and bacon. Bake 10 minutes more or until done. Makes one 9-inch meat pie.

TUNA POTATO BAKE

1 can (10¾ ounces)
condensed cream of
celery soup
⅓ cup water
¼ cup mayonnaise
2 tablespoons chopped
parsley
1 teaspoon lemon juice
⅛ teaspoon dry mustard

4 cups cubed cooked
potatoes
2 cans (about 7 ounces
each) tuna, drained and
flaked
3 slices (about 3 ounces)
mild process cheese,
cut in half diagonally

In 2-quart casserole, blend soup, water, mayonnaise, parsley, lemon juice, and mustard. Stir in potatoes and tuna. Bake at 400°F. for 30 minutes or until hot; stir. Top with cheese. Bake 5 minutes more or until cheese melts. Makes about 6 cups.

ADVANCED DEGREES: *How do you know when your oven is pre-heated? An oven thermometer tells you exactly. Otherwise, wait about 10 minutes. Most important: avoid pre-heating longer than necessary at a higher setting than called for. Dialing higher will not heat the oven faster. What's more, you just might forget to turn the setting back.*

stout-hearted skilletry

And Other Stove-Top Delights

Take one sturdy skillet, add the ingredients in the following recipes, and relax—some stick-to-the-ribs eating is on the way. Rustle up these robust dishes whenever you need something quick-to-fix and sure-to-please. Easy does it.

ALPINE MEATBALLS

½ pound ground beef
2 tablespoons fine dry
 bread crumbs
2 tablespoons finely
 chopped onion
¼ teaspoon salt
1 egg, slightly beaten
2 tablespoons shortening
1 can (10¾ ounces)
 condensed cream of
 mushroom soup

¼ cup water
¼ cup chopped canned
 tomatoes
2 tablespoons chopped
 parsley
¼ teaspoon basil leaves,
 crushed
2 cups cooked noodles
⅓ cup grated Parmesan
 cheese

In bowl, mix *thoroughly* beef, crumbs, onion, salt, and egg. Shape into 12 meatballs. In skillet, brown meatballs in shortening; pour off fat. Add soup, water, tomatoes, parsley, and basil. Cover; cook over low heat 20 minutes. Add noodles and cheese. Heat; stir occasionally. Makes about 4 cups.

ALL ABOARD! *Schedule your dishwasher for full loads only— once a day, if possible. Several meals-worth of dishes will make this appliance run farther on less—energy, detergent, water.*

BOLOGNA RICE COMBO

2 cups cubed bologna
¾ cup raw regular rice
1 cup sliced celery
2 tablespoons butter or
 margarine

1 can (10½ ounces)
 condensed onion soup
1 cup water

In skillet, brown bologna and rice and cook celery in butter until tender. Stir in soup and water; bring to boil. Reduce heat; cover. Cook over low heat 25 minutes or until rice is done. Stir occasionally. Makes about 4½ cups.

SASSY BEEF AND NOODLES

1 pound ground beef
1 medium onion, chopped
1 can (10¾ ounces)
    condensed cream of
    mushroom soup
¼ teaspoon hot pepper
    sauce
1 teaspoon salt
1 can (10½ ounces)
    condensed beef broth
1 cup water
3 cups uncooked medium
    noodles

In skillet, brown beef and cook onion until tender (use shortening if necessary). Stir to separate meat; pour off fat. Blend in mushroom soup, hot pepper sauce, and salt. Add remaining ingredients. Bring to boil; reduce heat. Cover; cook 10 minutes or until noodles are done. Stir often. Makes about 5 cups.

STUFFED CHICKEN ROLL-UPS

3 chicken breasts, split, skinned, and boned (about 1½ pounds boneless)
1 can (10¾ ounces) condensed cream of onion soup
1 cup small bread cubes
2 tablespoons chopped parsley
½ teaspoon oregano leaves, crushed
1 can (about 4 ounces) sliced mushrooms, drained
2 tablespoons butter or margarine
¼ cup water

Flatten chicken breasts with flat side of knife. To make stuffing, combine 3 tablespoons soup, bread cubes, parsley, and oregano. Place stuffing in center of each chicken breast. Roll up; tuck in ends. Secure with toothpicks. In skillet, brown chicken and mushrooms in butter. Add remaining soup and water. Cover; cook over low heat 20 minutes or until done. Stir occasionally. Makes 6 servings.

HAM AND TURKEY POLYNESIAN

½ cup diced cooked ham
½ cup green pepper strips
2 tablespoons butter or
   margarine
1 can (18¾ ounces)
   chunky turkey soup
¼ cup drained pineapple
   tidbits

¼ cup sliced water
   chestnuts
Dash salt
1 tablespoon cornstarch
2 tablespoons water
Cooked rice

In saucepan, brown ham and cook green pepper in butter until tender. Add soup, pineapple, water chestnuts, and salt. Blend cornstarch and water until smooth; add to soup mixture. Cook, stirring until thickened. Serve over rice. Makes about 3 cups.

SHOPPERS' ENEMY #1: Impulse buying. This scoundrel takes control of your arm and is extremely dangerous to your budget. To protect yourself, carry a shopping list at all times, eat before you shop, and leave the rest of the family at home (especially if they are the I want it types).

SKILLET CHICKEN BARBECUE

2 pounds chicken parts
2 tablespoons shortening
1 can (11 ounces)
   condensed tomato
   bisque soup
¼ cup chopped onion

2 teaspoons
   Worcestershire
½ teaspoon vinegar
Dash hot pepper sauce
1 package (9 ounces)
   frozen cut green beans

In skillet, brown chicken in shortening; pour off fat. Stir in remaining ingredients except beans. Cover; cook over low heat 30 minutes. Add beans. Cook 15 minutes more or until done. Stir occasionally. Makes 4 servings.

SKILLET STEAKS CASINO

1 pound boneless round steak (½-inch thick)	¾ cup water
2 tablespoons shortening	¼ cup chili sauce
1 can (10¾ ounces) condensed cream of onion soup	3 medium potatoes (about 1 pound), quartered
	1 package (9 ounces) frozen cut green beans

Pound steak; cut into serving-size pieces. In skillet, brown steak in shortening; pour off fat. Add soup, water, and chili sauce. Cover; cook over low heat 30 minutes. Add potatoes; cook 45 minutes more. Add beans. Cook 20 minutes more or until done; stir occasionally. Makes 4 servings.

DENIZENS OF THE DEEP FREEZE: *Wouldn't it be nice to know exactly who's who in your freezer without benefit of X-ray eyes? Easy. Mark all packages with tape and waxed pencil before freezing. Keep an up-to-date inventory sheet near the freezer that tells the location of every item. Soon you'll be wisking food out with such speed that warm air won't have a chance to get inside and run up operating costs.*

COWPOKE CASSOULET

1 pound ground beef	1 can (16 ounces) pork & beans with tomato sauce
1 medium onion, chopped	
1 can (11¼ ounces) condensed chili beef soup	¼ cup water

In skillet, brown beef and cook onion until tender (use shortening if necessary). Stir to separate meat; pour off fat. Add remaining ingredients. Heat; stir occasionally. Makes about 4½ cups.

MEATBALLS LA SCALA

½ pound ground beef
¼ teaspoon salt
Dash pepper
2 tablespoons shortening
1 can (19 ounces) chunky
   vegetable soup
½ cup uncooked thin
   spaghetti broken in pieces

1 small clove garlic,
   minced
¼ teaspoon Italian
   seasoning, crushed

Mix *thoroughly* beef, salt, and pepper. Shape into 16 meatballs. In saucepan, brown meatballs in shortening; pour off fat. Add remaining ingredients. Bring to boil; reduce heat. Cover; simmer 20 minutes or until done. Stir often. Makes about 3 cups.

SAUCY LIVER STRIPS

1 pound sliced beef liver,
   cut in strips
1 large clove garlic,
   minced
½ teaspoon oregano
   leaves, crushed

2 tablespoons butter or
   margarine
1 can (10¾ ounces)
   condensed tomato soup
¼ cup water
Cooked rice

In skillet, brown liver with garlic and oregano in butter. Add remaining ingredients except rice. Cover; cook over low heat 20 minutes or until done. Stir occasionally. Serve over rice. Makes about 2½ cups.

GOING BANANAS: *No need to let bananas get over-ripe and go uneaten. Ripen them to desired maturity at room temperature, then refrigerate until ready to use.*

If you do have over-ripe bananas on hand, that's the day to bake a banana quick-bread or cake—to eat, freeze, or give to a friend.

KLONDIKE CHICKEN

3-pound stewing chicken,
  cut up
Salt
Pepper
½ teaspoon paprika
2 tablespoons bacon
  drippings
2 medium green peppers,
  chopped
2 medium onions,
  chopped
1 can (10¾ ounces)
  condensed tomato soup
½ soup can water
1 cup diced cooked ham,
  sausage, or pork
¼ to ½ teaspoon red
  pepper flakes
½ teaspoon salt
Cooked rice

Season chicken with salt, pepper, and paprika. In large heavy pan, slowly brown chicken in bacon drippings (about 20 minutes); remove. Add green pepper and onion; cook until tender. Return chicken to pan; add remaining ingredients except rice. Cover; cook over low heat 35 minutes or until done. Stir occasionally. Skim excess fat from sauce; thicken if desired. Serve with rice. Makes 4 servings.

SPEEDY STROGANOFF

1 can (about 2 ounces)
  sliced mushrooms,
  drained
¼ cup chopped onion
2 tablespoons butter or
  margarine
1 can (19 ounces) chunky
  beef soup
¼ cup sour cream
1 cup cooked noodles
2 teaspoons paprika

In saucepan, brown mushrooms and cook onion in butter until tender. Add remaining ingredients. Heat; stir occasionally. Makes about 3 cups.

SAVORY STEW with DUMPLINGS

½ pound bulk sausage
2 cans (18¾ ounces each) chunky turkey soup
1 can (about 8 ounces) whole kernel golden corn, drained

⅛ teaspoon poultry seasoning
1 cup biscuit mix
⅓ cup milk
2 tablespoons chopped parsley

In saucepan, brown sausage; stir to separate meat. Pour off fat. Add soup, corn, and poultry seasoning. Bring to boil; stir occasionally. Meanwhile, combine biscuit mix, milk, and parsley. Drop 5 to 6 spoonfuls on boiling soup. Reduce heat; cook uncovered over low heat 10 minutes. Cover; cook 10 minutes more. Makes about 5½ cups.

JACK SPRAT DIDN'T KNOW WHAT HE WAS MISSING: Improve the flavor of your cooking and save money doing it. How? Collect beef and bacon fats in small jars, adding more as you go along. Store in refrigerator. Use them for sautéeing potatoes, onions, and vegetables; for browning stew meat; and for frying chicken.

DUTCH TREAT DINNER

2 frankfurters, sliced
¼ cup chopped onion
2 tablespoons butter or margarine
1 can (19 ounces) chunky split pea with ham soup

1 cup cooked elbow macaroni
2 tablespoons ketchup

In saucepan, brown frankfurters and cook onion in butter until tender. Add remaining ingredients. Heat; stir occasionally. Makes about 3 cups.

BURGERS ROMANESQUE

1 can (10¾ ounces)
   condensed cream of
   mushroom soup
1 pound ground beef
¼ cup fine dry bread
   crumbs
1 egg, slightly beaten
½ teaspoon salt

Generous dash pepper
2 cups sliced zucchini
½ cup sliced onion
½ cup drained chopped
   canned tomatoes
¼ teaspoon Italian
   seasoning, crushed
Dash garlic powder

Mix *thoroughly* ¼ cup soup, beef, bread crumbs, egg, salt, and pepper. Shape *firmly* into 4 patties. In skillet, brown patties (use shortening if necessary); pour off fat. Add remaining ingredients. Cover; cook over low heat 20 minutes or until done. Stir occasionally. Makes 4 servings.

CHICKEN ORIENT

1 pound fresh broccoli
2 tablespoons salad or
   peanut oil
2 whole chicken breasts
   (about 1½ pounds),
   split, skinned, boned,
   and cut in strips
¼ pound sliced fresh
   mushrooms (about 1
   cup)

1 can (10¾ ounces)
   condensed cream of
   chicken soup
½ cup coarsely chopped
   cashews or peanuts
½ cup water
¼ cup chopped pimiento

Remove flowerets from broccoli; break into small pieces. Peel stalk and cut into thin strips (1-inch long). Pour oil in electric wok* and preheat, uncovered, at medium heat about 2 minutes. Add chicken and cook in oil until white (about 5 minutes), stirring constantly. Push chicken up the side. Add broccoli flowerets and strips; cook 5 minutes, stirring constantly. Add additional oil if necessary. Push broccoli up the side. Add mushrooms; cook 1 minute, stirring constantly. Push mushrooms up the side. Stir in remaining ingredients. Heat; stir occasionally. Makes about 6 cups.

*A 10″ skillet may be substituted for a wok.

STOPWATCH BEEF 'n' NOODLE SKILLET

1 pound ground beef
1 medium onion, chopped
1 can (10½ ounces)
   condensed onion soup
1 to 1½ soup cans water
3 cups uncooked fine
   noodles
¼ cup chili sauce

In skillet, brown beef and cook onion until tender (use shortening if necessary). Stir to separate meat; pour off fat. Stir in remaining ingredients. Bring to boil; cover. Reduce heat; simmer 5 minutes or until noodles are done. Stir often. Makes about 5 cups.

WHEN IS A "SPECIAL" NOT SO SPECIAL? When the quality is poor. For instance, lean meat at regular price is a better buy than very fatty, bony meat on sale. Low price is not always high value.
  So be flexible. If you see something that's an even better buy than what's on your list, substitute, substitute, substitute.

CHINESE STEW

½ cup diced luncheon
   meat
1 cup diagonally sliced
   celery
2 tablespoons butter or
   margarine
1 can (19 ounces) chunky
   chicken with rice soup

2 tablespoons sliced
   green onions
1 tablespoon soy sauce
1 tablespoon cornstarch
2 tablespoons water
Chinese noodles

In saucepan, brown luncheon meat and cook celery in butter until tender. Add soup, onion, and soy. Blend cornstarch and water until smooth; add to soup mixture. Cook, stirring until thickened. Serve over noodles with additional soy. Makes about 3 cups.

COUPONS, COUPONS, COUPONS: Cents off *coupons are great for items that you normally buy or have been wanting to try. But think: do you really need it? If not, it's no bargain, even with a coupon.*

CHICKEN SORRENTO

2 pounds chicken parts
2 tablespoons shortening
1 can (10½ ounces)
   condensed consommé
½ cup chopped canned
   tomatoes
1 medium onion,
   quartered

½ teaspoon oregano
   leaves, crushed
¼ teaspoon salt
Generous dash pepper
¼ cup water
2 tablespoons flour
Cooked rice or noodles

In skillet, brown chicken in shortening; pour off fat. Add consommé, tomatoes, onion, and seasonings. Cover; cook over low heat 45 minutes or until done. Gradually blend water into flour until smooth; slowly stir into sauce. Cook, stirring until thickened. Serve with rice. Makes 4 servings.

QUICK SKILLET STEW

1 can (about 16 ounces)
   small whole white
   potatoes
1 can (11 ounces)
   condensed Cheddar
   cheese soup
1 can (12 ounces)
   luncheon meat, cubed

1 can (about 8 ounces)
   sliced carrots, drained
2 tablespoons instant
   minced onion
½ teaspoon prepared
   mustard
⅛ teaspoon garlic powder

Drain potatoes, reserving ⅓ cup liquid; slice. In skillet, combine potatoes and reserved liquid with remaining ingredients. Heat; gently stir occasionally. Makes about 5 cups.

Fanciful Franks—recipe page 42

PEA PATCH CHICKEN

2 pounds chicken parts
2 tablespoons shortening
1 can (10¾ ounces)
  condensed golden
  mushroom soup

1 cup sliced onion
½ teaspoon salt
1 package (10 ounces)
  frozen peas, cooked
  and drained

In skillet, brown chicken in shortening; pour off fat. Stir in soup, onion, and salt. Cover; cook over low heat 45 minutes or until done. Stir occasionally. Add peas; heat. Makes 4 servings.

APRICOT PORK CHOPS

1 can (about 8 ounces)
  unpeeled apricot halves
6 pork chops (about 1½
  pounds)
1 can (10¾ ounces)
  condensed cream of
  chicken soup

⅓ cup sour cream
2 tablespoons chopped
  green onions
Cooked rice or noodles

Drain apricots reserving ¼ cup syrup. Cut apricots in half. In skillet, brown chops (use shortening if necessary); pour off fat. Stir in soup, sour cream, reserved syrup, and green onions. Cover; cook over low heat 25 minutes or until done. Stir occasionally. Add apricots; cook 5 minutes more. Serve with rice. Makes 4 servings.

BEEF AND POTATOES AU GRATIN

1 pound ground beef
1 medium onion, chopped
1 can (11 ounces)
  condensed Cheddar
  cheese soup

⅓ cup water
1 can (about 16 ounces)
  small whole white
  potatoes, drained and
  sliced

In skillet, brown beef and cook onion until tender (use shortening if necessary). Stir to separate meat; pour off fat. Blend in soup and water; add potatoes. Heat; stir occasionally. Makes about 4 cups.

Stuffed Shells Neapolitan—recipe page 72

MEATBALLS DIABLO

1 can (10¾ ounces)
  condensed cream of
  mushroom soup
1 pound ground beef
1 egg, slightly beaten
¼ cup fine dry bread
  crumbs
¼ cup finely chopped
  onion
1 tablespoon prepared
  mustard
1 tablespoon
  Worcestershire

2 teaspoons prepared
  horseradish
½ cup water

Mix *thoroughly* ¼ cup soup and remaining ingredients except water. Shape into 16 meatballs. In skillet, brown meatballs (use shortening if necessary); pour off fat. Stir in remaining soup and water. Cover; cook over low heat 20 minutes or until done. Stir occasionally. Makes about 3½ cups.

SAUCY LINKS

1 package (8 ounces)
  brown 'n serve sausage
  links
1 can (10¾ ounces)
  condensed cream of
  mushroom or celery
  soup
½ cup milk

½ teaspoon prepared
  mustard
2 tablespoons chopped
  parsley
2 cups sliced cooked
  potatoes
1 cup sliced cooked
  carrots

In skillet, brown sausage; pour off fat. Stir in soup, milk, mustard, and parsley. Add potatoes and carrots. Heat; stir occasionally. Makes about 4 cups.

LABELS ARE A SHOPPER'S BEST FRIEND! *Read them to find net weight, price, grade, product description, ingredients (listed by weight in descending order) and suggestions for preparation.*

EASY BURGOO

4 link sausage (about ½ pound)
2 pounds chicken parts
1 can (10¾ ounces) condensed cream of chicken soup
½ cup chopped onion
1 small clove garlic, minced
¼ teaspoon rubbed sage
1 can (15½ ounces) kidney beans, drained
2 medium zucchini, cut in ½-inch slices (about 2 cups)

In skillet, slowly brown sausage; remove. Pour off all but 2 tablespoons drippings. Brown chicken in drippings; pour off fat. Add soup, onion, garlic, sage, and sausage. Cover; cook over low heat 30 minutes. Add beans and zucchini. Cook 15 minutes more or until done. Stir occasionally. Makes 4 servings.

LIGHTNING SPAGHETTI

1 pound ground beef
1 medium onion, chopped
1 can (10¾ ounces) condensed tomato soup
1 can (15 ounces) spaghetti in tomato sauce with cheese
Grated Parmesan cheese

In skillet, brown beef and cook onion until tender (use shortening if necessary). Stir to separate meat; pour off fat. Add soup and spaghetti. Heat; stir occasionally. Serve with cheese. Makes about 4½ cups.

GREAT GOULASH

1½ pounds sirloin beef cubes (1 inch)
2 tablespoons shortening
1 can (10¾ ounces) condensed golden mushroom soup
1 teaspoon paprika
½ cup sour cream
Cooked noodles

In skillet, brown beef in shortening; pour off fat. Blend in soup and paprika. Cover; cook over low heat 1 hour or until done. Stir occasionally. Gradually stir in sour cream; heat. Serve over noodles. Makes about 3 cups.

GOLD COAST PORK CHOPS

6 pork chops (about 1½ pounds)
1 can (10¾ ounces) condensed golden mushroom soup
¼ cup water
1 cup carrots thinly sliced diagonally
½ cup chopped onion
Generous dash rubbed sage
1 small green pepper, cut in strips

In skillet, brown chops (use shortening if necessary); pour off fat. Stir in soup, water, carrots, onion, and sage. Cover; cook over low heat 15 minutes. Add green pepper; cook 15 minutes more or until done. Stir occasionally. Makes 4 servings.

TIAJUANA PORK CHOPS

6 pork chops (about 1½ pounds)
1 can (10¾ ounces) condensed cream of celery soup
1 teaspoon chili powder
⅛ teaspoon garlic salt
1 cup canned chick peas
1 cup green pepper squares (1 inch)

In skillet, brown chops (use shortening if necessary); pour off fat. Add soup, chili, and garlic salt. Cover; cook over low heat 15 minutes. Add peas and pepper. Cook 15 minutes more or until done; stir occasionally. Makes 4 servings.

MASON-DIXON SUPPER

1 can (12 ounces) luncheon meat, cubed
⅓ cup diagonally sliced celery
¼ cup chopped onion
2 tablespoons butter or margarine
1 can (10¾ ounces) condensed chicken broth
¾ cup water
¾ cup raw regular rice
1 can (about 8 ounces) sliced peaches, drained

In saucepan, brown luncheon meat and cook celery and onion in butter until tender. Stir in broth, water, and rice. Bring to boil; reduce heat. Cover; cook 20 minutes or until rice is done. Stir occasionally. Add peaches; heat. Makes about 4½ cups.

HOT DEVILED EGGS

4 slices bacon
6 hard-cooked eggs
1 can (10¾ ounces)
   condensed cream of
   chicken soup
⅛ teaspoon dry mustard
Generous dash pepper
1 can (about 4 ounces)
   sliced mushrooms,
   drained

½ cup water
¼ cup shredded sharp
   Cheddar cheese
1 tablespoon dried chives
4 English muffins, split
   and toasted

In skillet, cook bacon until crisp; remove and crumble. Pour off all but 2 tablespoons drippings. Meanwhile, cut eggs in half lengthwise; carefully remove and mash yolks. Mix yolks with 2 tablespoons soup, crumbled bacon, mustard, and pepper. Fill egg whites with yolk mixture. In skillet, lightly brown mushrooms in drippings. Add remaining soup, water, cheese, and chives. Arrange eggs in soup mixture. Cover; cook over low heat until eggs are hot and cheese melts. Stir gently, spooning sauce over eggs. Serve on muffins. Makes 4 servings.

CHINESE SUPPER SKILLET

1 pound ground beef
1 medium onion, chopped
2 cans (10¾ ounces each)
   condensed golden
   mushroom soup
½ cup water
1 can (16 ounces) Chinese
   vegetables, drained
1 cup quick-cooking rice,
   uncooked
1 teaspoon soy sauce

In skillet, brown beef and cook onion until tender (use shortening if necessary). Stir to separate meat; pour off fat. Add remaining ingredients; bring to boil. Cover. Reduce heat; cook 10 minutes or until rice is done. Stir often. Serve with additional soy. Makes about 6 cups.

MAKING A LIST, CHECKING IT TWICE: *Your budget will think you're Santa Claus if you acquire the habit of shopping with a list.*

First, scan newspapers for advertised specials. Then plan menus for at least a week around bargains that the family enjoys.

Next, check pantry and refrigerator/freezer for needed items. And finally, make a detailed shopping list according to store layout.

SKILLET STEAK AND RICE

1½ pounds boneless round steak (¾-inch thick)
2 tablespoons shortening
1 can (10¾ ounces) condensed golden mushroom soup
1 cup water
½ cup Burgundy or other dry red wine
½ cup sliced onion
¼ teaspoon salt
1½ cups quick-cooking rice, uncooked
1 package (10 ounces) frozen Brussels sprouts, cooked and drained

Pound steak; cut into serving-size pieces. In skillet, brown steak in shortening; pour off fat. Add soup, water, wine, onion, and salt. Cover; cook over low heat 1 hour 15 minutes. Stir occasionally. Add rice and Brussels sprouts; bring to boil. Reduce heat; cover. Cook 10 minutes or until done. Makes 4 servings.

LOUISIANA CHICKEN

2 slices bacon
½ cup chopped onion
1 small green pepper, sliced
⅛ teaspoon thyme leaves, crushed
1 can (10¾ ounces) condensed tomato soup
½ cup water
1½ cups diced cooked chicken
Cooked rice

In skillet, cook bacon until crisp; remove and crumble. Cook onion and pepper with thyme in bacon drippings until tender. Stir in soup, water, and chicken. Heat; stir occasionally. Serve over rice. Garnish with bacon. Makes about 3 cups.

HAMBURGER RISOTTO

1 pound ground beef
½ cup chopped onion
1 can (10¾ ounces)
  condensed tomato soup
1½ cups water
1½ cups quick-cooking
  rice, uncooked
1 medium clove garlic,
  minced

1 teaspoon oregano
  leaves, crushed
1 teaspoon salt
3 medium zucchini (about
  ¾ pound), cut in ¼-inch
  slices
Grated Parmesan cheese

In skillet, brown beef and cook onion until tender (use shortening if necessary); stir to separate meat. Pour off fat. Add remaining ingredients except cheese. Bring to boil; cover. Reduce heat; simmer 10 minutes or until rice is done. Stir often. Serve with Parmesan. Makes about 6 cups.

SAUSAGE SKILLET ROMA

2 medium zucchini (about
  ½ pound), cut in half
  lengthwise
1 pound bulk sausage
1 can (10¾ ounces)
  condensed cream of
  mushroom soup

½ cup thinly sliced onion
1 medium clove garlic,
  minced
1 medium tomato, cut in
  wedges

Cut squash into 1-inch pieces. Shape sausage into 16 meatballs. In skillet, brown sausage; pour off fat. Add remaining ingredients except tomato. Cover; cook over low heat 15 minutes or until done. Stir occasionally. Add tomatoes; cook 5 minutes more. Makes about 4 cups.

FLOUR POWER: *Keep flour in an airtight container since it tends to absorb odors, take up moisture, and dry out easily, depending on conditions.*

To avoid unwanted guests—insects—store in a cool place.

Whole wheat flour? Give it a home in the refrigerator since natural oils cause it to turn rancid quickly at room temperature.

FANCIFUL FRANKS

½ pound frankfurters, cut in 1-inch pieces
½ cup chopped onion
1 teaspoon oregano leaves, crushed
2 tablespoons butter or margarine
1 can (11¼ ounces) condensed chili beef soup
1 can (15 ounces) spaghetti in tomato sauce with cheese

In saucepan, brown frankfurters and cook onion with oregano in butter until tender. Stir in soup and spaghetti. Heat; stir occasionally. Makes about 3½ cups.

HAM AND SAUSAGE MEDLEY

8 link sausage (about ½ pound)
1 can (10½ ounces) condensed beef broth
1 cup cubed cooked ham
½ cup raw regular rice
½ cup chopped canned tomatoes
1 small clove garlic, minced
1 package (9 ounces) frozen cut green beans

In skillet, brown sausage. Pour off fat. Add remaining ingredients except beans. Bring to boil; reduce heat. Cover; cook 10 minutes. Add beans; cook 10 minutes more or until done. Stir occasionally. Makes about 4 cups.

CHILI CHOPS

6 pork chops (about 1½ pounds)
Salt
Pepper
1 can (10¾ ounces) condensed tomato soup
1 can (15½ ounces) kidney beans, undrained
½ cup sliced onion
1 tablespoon chili powder
1 large clove garlic, minced
6 green pepper rings
Cooked rice

In skillet, brown chops (use shortening if necessary); pour off fat. Season with salt and pepper. Add remaining ingredients except green pepper and rice. Cover; cook over low heat 15 minutes. Top each chop with green pepper ring. Cook 15 minutes more or until done. Stir occasionally. Serve with rice. Makes 4 servings.

POACHED EGGS LUMBERJACK STYLE

1 pound ground beef
1 medium onion, chopped
2 cans (10¾ ounces each)
  condensed cream of
  potato soup
¼ cup water
⅛ teaspoon celery salt
4 eggs

In skillet, brown beef and cook onion until tender (use shortening if necessary); stir to separate meat. Pour off fat. Blend in soup, water, and celery salt; bring to boil. Gently slip eggs into soup mixture. Cover; cook over low heat until whites are firm. Makes 4 servings.

CHICKEN SKILLET GARNI

2 pounds chicken legs
2 tablespoons shortening
1 can (10¾ ounces)
  condensed cream of
  chicken soup
⅛ teaspoon ground thyme

½ cup diced carrots
¼ cup chopped celery
¼ cup sliced green onions
¼ cup chopped green
  pepper

In skillet, brown chicken in shortening; pour off fat. Add soup and thyme. Cover; cook over low heat 15 minutes. Add remaining ingredients. Cook 30 minutes more or until done. Stir occasionally. Makes 4 servings.

SAUSAGE CABBAGE SKILLET

1 pound mild Italian
  sausage, cut in 1-inch
  pieces
1 can (10¾ ounces)
  condensed tomato soup
1 soup can water
2 cups coarsely chopped
  cabbage

1 package (9 ounces)
  frozen cut green beans
½ teaspoon basil leaves,
  crushed
⅛ teaspoon garlic salt
½ cup uncooked elbow
  macaroni

In skillet, brown sausage; pour off fat. Add remaining ingredients. Bring to boil; reduce heat. Cover; simmer 20 minutes or until done. Stir often. Makes about 5½ cups.

PORK CHOPS JARDINIER

6 pork chops (about 1½
   pounds)
1 can (10¾ ounces)
   condensed cream of
   mushroom soup
¼ cup water
⅛ teaspoon pepper

⅛ teaspoon thyme leaves,
   crushed
1 can (about 16 ounces)
   lima beans, drained
½ cup drained chopped
   canned tomatoes

In skillet, brown chops; pour off fat. Add soup, water, and
seasonings. Cover; cook over low heat 30 minutes or until
done. Stir occasionally. Add beans and tomatoes; heat.
Makes 4 servings.

CHICKEN CROQUETTES

1 can (10¾ ounces)
   condensed cream of
   chicken soup
1½ cups finely chopped
   cooked chicken
¼ cup fine dry bread
   crumbs
2 tablespoons finely
   chopped celery

1 tablespoon finely
   chopped onion
¼ teaspoon poultry
   seasoning
Shortening
½ cup milk

To make croquettes, combine ⅓ cup soup, chicken, bread
crumbs, celery, onion, and ⅛ teaspoon poultry seasoning.
Mix well; shape into 6 croquettes or patties (if mixture is
difficult to handle, chill before shaping). Roll in additional
bread crumbs. In skillet, brown croquettes in shortening.
Meanwhile, in saucepan, combine remaining soup, ⅛
teaspoon poultry seasoning, and milk. Heat; stir occasionally. Serve with croquettes. Makes 3 servings.

FOIL THAT SPOIL: *Wash fresh fruit and mushrooms before
eating—not before storing. Moisture encourages spoilage. Store
in refrigerator in crisper or moisture-resistant wrap or containers.*

SPAGHETTI with MEAT SAUCE

½ pound ground beef
1 cup chopped onion
1 teaspoon basil leaves, crushed
1 teaspoon oregano leaves, crushed
1 large clove garlic, minced
1 can (10¾ ounces) condensed golden mushroom soup
1 can (10¾ ounces) condensed tomato soup
1 can (16 ounces) tomatoes
¼ cup water
Cooked spaghetti
Grated Parmesan cheese

In saucepan, brown beef and cook onion with seasonings until tender (use shortening if necessary); stir to separate meat. Add soups, tomatoes, and water. Stir to break up tomatoes. Simmer 30 minutes; stir occasionally. Serve over spaghetti with Parmesan. Makes about 4½ cups.

MEXICAN FRICASSEE

½ cup chopped green pepper
½ cup chopped onion
2 tablespoons butter or margarine
1 can (11¼ ounces) condensed chili beef soup
1 can (10¾ ounces) condensed tomato soup
½ cup water
2 cups cubed cooked beef
Cooked rice
Shredded Cheddar cheese

In saucepan, cook green pepper and onion in butter until tender. Stir in soups, water, and beef. Heat; stir occasionally. Serve on rice. Garnish with cheese. Makes about 5 cups.

TO MARKET, TO MARKET, BUT NOT TOO OFTEN: Each trip to the store means money spent for gas and another opportunity to buy extras that catch your eye. So shop as infrequently as your freezer and cupboard space allow.

LEFT BANK CHICKEN

3 pounds chicken parts
3 tablespoons shortening
2 cans (11 ounces each)
   condensed Cheddar
   cheese soup
1 can (16 ounces)
   tomatoes, drained and
   chopped
1 cup sliced onion
1 teaspoon dried dill
   weed, crushed
1 teaspoon salt
1 package (9 ounces)
   frozen cut green beans
1 package (10 ounces)
   frozen cauliflower
¼ cup water
1 to 2 tablespoons flour
Cooked noodles

In large heavy pan, brown chicken in shortening; pour off fat. Add soup, tomatoes, onion, and seasonings. Cover; cook over low heat 25 minutes. Add beans and cauliflower; cook 20 minutes more or until done. Stir occasionally. Remove chicken and vegetables to serving dish. Gradually blend water into flour until smooth; slowly stir into sauce. Cook, stirring until thickened. Serve with chicken mixture and noodles. Makes 6 servings.

CHICKEN PAPRIKA

2 pounds chicken parts
2 tablespoons shortening
1 can (10¾ ounces)
   condensed cream of
   chicken soup

1 tablespoon lemon juice
½ teaspoon paprika

In skillet, brown chicken in shortening; pour off fat. Stir in remaining ingredients. Cover; cook over low heat 45 minutes or until done. Stir occasionally. Makes 4 servings.

TALLYHO MEATBALLS

1 pound ground beef
½ pound liverwurst
1 egg, slightly beaten
1 slice white bread, crumbled
¼ cup finely chopped onion
Generous dash pepper
4 slices bacon
1 can (10¾ ounces) condensed cream of mushroom soup
⅓ cup water
½ cup sour cream

Mix *thoroughly* beef, liverwurst, egg, bread, onion, and pepper; shape into 24 meatballs. In skillet, cook bacon until crisp; remove and crumble. Brown meatballs in drippings; pour off fat. Stir in soup and water. Cover; cook over low heat 15 minutes. Stir in sour cream and bacon; cook 5 minutes more or until done. Stir occasionally. Makes about 4 cups.

FIVE O'CLOCK FRANKS

1 pound frankfurters, cut in thirds
½ cup chopped onion
2 tablespoons butter or margarine
1 can (11 ounces) condensed Cheddar cheese soup
⅓ cup water
2 cups cooked noodles
1 package (9 ounces) frozen cut green beans, cooked and drained
2 tablespoons ketchup

In skillet, brown frankfurters and cook onion in butter until tender. Add remaining ingredients. Heat; stir occasionally. Makes about 6 cups.

CHICKEN HAWAIIAN

2 whole chicken breasts (about 1½ pounds), split
2 tablespoons shortening
1 can (10¾ ounces) condensed cream of chicken soup
¼ cup water
½ cup green pepper strips
½ cup thinly sliced green onions
½ cup drained pineapple chunks
⅛ teaspoon ground ginger

In skillet, brown chicken in shortening; pour off fat. Add remaining ingredients. Cover; cook over low heat 30 minutes or until done. Makes 4 servings.

SUNSHINE CHICKEN

2 pounds chicken parts
2 tablespoons shortening
1 can (10¾ ounces)
   condensed golden
   mushroom soup

⅓ cup drained chopped
   canned tomatoes
½ cup sliced onion
⅛ teaspoon basil leaves,
   crushed
Cooked rice

In skillet, brown chicken in shortening; pour off fat. Add remaining ingredients except rice. Cover; cook over low heat 45 minutes or until done. Stir occasionally. Serve with rice. Makes 4 servings.

GERMAN STUFFED PORK CHOPS

¼ cup finely chopped
   onion
1 medium clove garlic,
   minced
2 tablespoons butter or
   margarine
1 cup dry rye bread cubes
¼ cup chopped parsley
4 thick pork chops (about
   1½ pounds)

1 can (10¾ ounces)
   condensed golden
   mushroom soup
½ cup sour cream
¼ cup water
⅛ teaspoon caraway seed
1 medium apple, cut in
   eighths

To make stuffing, in saucepan, cook onion with garlic in butter until tender; add bread and parsley. Trim excess fat from chops. Slit each chop from outer edge toward bone making a pocket; stuff with bread mixture. Fasten with toothpicks or skewers. In skillet, brown chops (use shortening if necessary); pour off fat. Blend in soup, sour cream, water, and caraway. Cover; cook over low heat 1 hour 15 minutes or until done; stir occasionally. Add apple; heat. Makes 4 servings.

SALISBURY STEAK

1 can (10½ ounces)
    condensed onion soup
1½ pounds ground beef
½ cup fine dry bread
    crumbs
1 egg, slightly beaten
¼ teaspoon salt
Dash pepper
¼ cup ketchup

1 teaspoon
    Worcestershire
½ teaspoon prepared
    mustard
¼ cup water
1 tablespoon flour

Mix *thoroughly* ⅓ cup soup, beef, bread crumbs, egg, salt, and pepper. Shape into 6 oval patties. In skillet, brown patties (use shortening if necessary); pour off fat. Add remaining soup, ketchup, Worcestershire, and mustard. Gradually blend water into flour until smooth. Stir into soup mixture. Cover; cook over low heat 20 minutes or until done. Stir occasionally. Makes 6 servings.

TANGY POTATO MEATBALLS

1 can (10¾ ounces)
    condensed tomato soup
1 pound ground beef
½ cup instant mashed
    potato flakes or puffs
1 egg, slightly beaten
¼ cup finely chopped
    onion

1 teaspoon salt
1 tablespoon shortening
¼ cup water
1 teaspoon prepared
    mustard
1 small clove garlic,
    minced

Mix *thoroughly* ¼ cup soup, beef, potato flakes, egg, onion, and salt. Shape *firmly* into 16 meatballs. Brown meatballs in shortening; pour off fat. Blend in remaining soup, water, mustard, and garlic. Cover; cook over low heat 20 minutes or until done. Stir occasionally. Makes about 4 cups.

GRECIAN LAMB SKILLET

2 cups cubed eggplant
(½ medium)
⅓ cup chopped green
pepper
1 medium clove garlic,
minced
¼ teaspoon thyme leaves,
crushed

2 tablespoons butter or
margarine
1 can (10¾ ounces)
condensed tomato soup
1 soup can water
1½ cups cooked lamb cut
in strips
1⅓ cups quick-cooking
rice, uncooked

In skillet, cook eggplant and green pepper with garlic and thyme in butter until tender. Add remaining ingredients. Bring to boil; reduce heat. Cover; cook 10 minutes or until rice is done. Stir occasionally. Makes about 5½ cups.

MILK AND MONEY: Non fat dry milk costs about half as much as fluid whole milk, so your money-saving strategy is easy:
*Keep a supply of reconstituted non fat dry milk in the refrigerator **for cooking** (you can't tell the difference) and **for drinking** (the secret is keep it COLD). Or mix equal parts of whole milk and reconstituted dry milk if that suits your beverage tastebuds better.*

CHICKEN CRÉCY

2 pounds chicken parts
2 tablespoons shortening
1 can (10¾ ounces)
condensed golden
mushroom soup

1 cup sliced carrots
½ cup chopped onion
⅛ teaspoon ground
nutmeg

In skillet, brown chicken in shortening; pour off fat. Add remaining ingredients. Cover; cook over low heat 45 minutes or until done. Stir occasionally. Makes 4 servings.

PORK CHOPS WITH PIZZAZ

6 pork chops (about 1½ pounds), well-trimmed
Salt
Pepper
1 can (10¾ ounces) condensed chicken broth
¼ teaspoon hot pepper sauce
3 cups uncooked fine noodles, broken in pieces
1 cup chopped canned tomatoes

In skillet, brown chops (use shortening if necessary); pour off fat. Season with salt and pepper. Add broth and hot pepper sauce. Cover; cook over low heat 15 minutes. Add noodles and tomatoes; cook 15 minutes more or until done. Stir often. Makes 4 servings.

ONION STEAK

¼ cup flour
¼ teaspoon salt
Dash pepper
1½ pounds round steak (¾-inch thick)
2 tablespoons shortening
1 can (10½ ounces) condensed onion soup
½ cup ketchup
1 medium green pepper, cut in strips

Combine flour and seasonings; pound into steak. Cut steak into serving-size pieces. In skillet, brown steak in shortening; pour off fat. Add soup and ketchup. Cover; cook over low heat 1 hour 15 minutes. Add green pepper; cook 15 minutes more or until done. Stir occasionally. Makes 4 servings.

CHILI BEEF HASH

1 pound ground beef
3 cups diced raw potatoes
1 cup sliced celery
2 tablespoons shortening
1 can (10¾ ounces) condensed golden mushroom soup
½ cup water
¼ cup chili sauce
½ teaspoon salt
Generous dash pepper

In skillet, brown beef and cook potatoes and celery in shortening; stir to separate meat. Pour off fat. Add remaining ingredients. Cover; cook over low heat 10 minutes. Stir occasionally. Makes about 4½ cups.

CHICKEN SALERNO

¼ pound mild Italian
  sausage, sliced
1 cup zucchini slices cut in
  half
1 small clove garlic,
  minced
1 can (19 ounces) chunky
  chicken soup

½ cup drained chopped
  canned tomatoes
1 tablespoon cornstarch
2 tablespoons water
Italian bread slices,
  toasted
Grated Parmesan cheese

In saucepan, cook sausage until done; add zucchini and garlic. Cook until zucchini is tender. Add soup and tomatoes. Blend cornstarch and water; add to soup mixture. Cook over low heat, stirring until thickened. Serve over Italian bread sprinkled with cheese. Makes about 3 cups.

CHEESE-SMOTHERED CHICKEN

2 pounds chicken parts
2 tablespoons butter or
  margarine
1 can (11 ounces)
  condensed Cheddar
  cheese soup

½ cup cut-up canned
  tomatoes
⅓ cup finely chopped
  onion
¼ teaspoon basil leaves,
  crushed

In skillet, slowly brown chicken in butter (about 30 minutes). Add remaining ingredients. Cover; cook over low heat 15 minutes or until done. Stir occasionally. Makes 4 servings.

TIGHT FIT: Are the gaskets around your refrigerator and freezer doors worn out or ill-fitting? If so, they can run up operating costs by letting cold air out and warm air in.

To test for tightness, place a dollar bill between the gasket and the cabinet. Close the door normally. Pull the dollar bill straight out—there should be at least a slight drag.

Test all around the door, including the side hinge. No drag in places? Call a serviceman to check the gasket and door for alignment.

INDIVIDUAL CANTONESE STEAKS

1½ pounds boneless
  round steak (¾-inch
  thick)
2 tablespoons shortening
1 can (10½ ounces)
  condensed beef broth
¾ cup water

1 tablespoon soy sauce
1 large green pepper, cut
  in strips
3 tablespoons cornstarch
Cooked rice

Cut meat into serving-size pieces. In skillet, brown meat in shortening; pour off fat. Add broth, ½ cup water, and soy. Cover; cook over low heat 1 hour 15 minutes. Add green pepper; cook 10 minutes more or until done. Stir occasionally. Blend ¼ cup water and cornstarch until smooth; slowly stir into sauce. Cook, stirring until thickened. Serve with rice and additional soy. Makes 4 servings.

SPICY HOT CHICKEN SKILLET

2 pounds chicken parts
2 tablespoons shortening
1 can (10¾ ounces)
  condensed tomato soup
¼ cup water
1 cup sliced onion
1 large clove garlic,
  minced
2 teaspoons chili powder

⅛ teaspoon ground
  cinnamon
Generous dash crushed
  red pepper
¼ cup sliced pimiento-
  stuffed olives
1 large green pepper, cut
  in strips
Cooked rice

In skillet, brown chicken in shortening; pour off fat. Add remaining ingredients except olives, green pepper, and rice. Cover; cook over low heat 35 minutes. Add olives and green pepper. Cook 10 minutes more or until done. Stir occasionally. Serve with rice. Makes 4 servings.

THE HUNGRY EYE: Never shop on an empty stomach. Studies show that the hungry shopper sees more that looks appealing and buys accordingly—with budget-battering results.

CHICKEN ZUCCHINI SKILLET

2 pounds chicken parts
2 tablespoons shortening
1 can (10¾ ounces)
   condensed cream of
   mushroom soup
½ cup well-drained
   chopped canned
   tomatoes

1 medium clove garlic,
   minced
⅛ teaspoon Italian
   seasoning, crushed
2 medium zucchini, sliced
   (about 1 pound)
Cooked rice
Grated Parmesan cheese

In skillet, brown chicken in shortening; pour off fat. Add soup, tomatoes, garlic, and seasoning. Cover; cook over low heat 30 minutes. Add squash; cook 15 minutes more or until done. Stir occasionally. Uncover; cook to desired consistency. Serve with rice; garnish with cheese. Makes 4 servings.

TEXAS MEATBALLS

1 pound ground beef
½ pound bulk sausage
½ cup soft bread crumbs
1 egg, slightly beaten
1 can (10½ ounces)
   condensed onion soup
1 can (10¾ ounces)
   condensed tomato soup
2 tablespoons cornstarch
2 large cloves garlic,
   minced

¼ cup vinegar
3 tablespoons brown
   sugar
1 tablespoon
   Worcestershire
⅛ teaspoon hot pepper
   sauce
Cooked rice

Mix *thoroughly* beef, sausage, crumbs, and egg. Shape into 24 meatballs. In skillet, brown meatballs; pour off fat. Add remaining ingredients except rice. Cover; cook over low heat 20 minutes or until done. Stir occasionally. Serve with rice. Makes about 5 cups.

AND THE COST CAME TUMBLING DOWN: *You'll be able to spot genuine bargain prices instantly if you keep a week to week list of regular food prices until you become very familiar with them.*

RED FLANNEL PORK HASH

2 cups diced cooked pork
½ cup chopped onion
⅓ cup salad oil
1 package (16 ounces)
   frozen hash brown
   potatoes
½ teaspoon salt
Generous dash pepper

1 can (10¾ ounces)
   condensed cream of
   chicken soup
1 jar (16 ounces) pickled
   beets, drained and
   chopped
¼ cup chopped parsley
Sliced hard-cooked egg

In skillet, brown pork and cook onion in 2 tablespoons oil until tender. Add remaining oil, potatoes, salt, and pepper. Cook 10 minutes. Stir in soup, beets, and parsley. Heat; stir occasionally. Garnish with egg and additional parsley. Makes about 5 cups.

BURGERS 'n' VEGETABLES

1 pound ground beef
¼ cup finely chopped
   onion
½ teaspoon salt
Generous dash pepper
1 can (10¾ ounces)
   condensed golden
   mushroom soup

¼ cup water
1 teaspoon
   Worcestershire
1 cup thinly sliced carrots
1 package (9 ounces)
   frozen cut green beans

Mix *thoroughly* beef, onion, salt, and pepper; shape *firmly* into 4 oval patties. In skillet, brown patties (use shortening if necessary); pour off fat. Stir in remaining ingredients. Cover; cook over low heat 20 minutes or until done. Stir occasionally. Makes 4 servings.

PUT YOUR DISHWASHER ON A MAINTENANCE DIET: *Scrape excess food from plates before your dishwasher has a chance to devour it. Debris in the pump can hamper the machine's efficiency. Also, check the filter screen over the drain in the dishwasher regularly and remove any particles.*

FRANKFURTER EXPRESS

½ pound frankfurters, cut
  in ½-inch slices
1 small onion, sliced
2 tablespoons butter or
  margarine
1 can (10¾ ounces)
  condensed cream of
  mushroom soup

¼ cup water
1 can (16 ounces) small
  whole white potatoes,
  drained and diced
1 can (8 ounces) cut green
  beans, drained

In saucepan, brown frankfurters and cook onion in butter until tender. Add soup, water, potatoes, and green beans. Heat; stir occasionally. Makes about 4 cups.

IS THERE A PEEP-SHOW IN YOUR KITCHEN? If you can't resist looking in the oven every time something is cooking, there is. And the price of admission is a higher utility bill; all that escaping heat mounts up.

CHEESY TUNA MEDLEY

2 slices bacon
¼ cup sliced green onions
⅛ teaspoon thyme leaves,
  crushed
1 can (11 ounces)
  condensed Cheddar
  cheese soup

2 tablespoons water
½ cup drained cut-up
  canned tomatoes
Generous dash pepper
2 cups sliced cooked
  potatoes
2 cans (about 7 ounces
  each) tuna, drained and
  flaked

In saucepan, cook bacon until crisp; remove and crumble. Pour off all but 2 tablespoons drippings. Cook onion with thyme in drippings until tender. Stir in soup, water, tomatoes, and pepper; add potatoes and tuna. Heat; stir occasionally. Garnish with bacon. Makes about 4½ cups.

MEATBALLS NAPOLI

1 pound meatloaf mix
¼ cup fine dry bread
   crumbs
¼ cup finely chopped
   onion
1 egg, slightly beaten
¼ teaspoon salt
Generous dash pepper
1 can (10¾ ounces)
   condensed cream of
   chicken soup

1 can (16 ounces)
   tomatoes, chopped
   and drained
¼ teaspoon Italian
   seasoning, crushed
Cooked rice

In bowl, mix *thoroughly* meat, bread crumbs, onion, egg, salt, and pepper. Shape into 16 meatballs. In skillet, brown meatballs (use shortening if necessary); pour off fat. Stir in soup, tomatoes, and seasoning. Cover; cook over low heat 20 minutes or until done. Stir occasionally. Serve with rice. Makes about 4 cups.

SAUSAGE CHUCKWAGON STYLE

1 can (11¼ ounces)
   condensed chili beef
   soup
1 can (about 16 ounces)
   whole green beans

⅔ cup raw regular rice
¼ teaspoon onion salt
2 cans (5 ounces each)
   Vienna sausage,
   drained

In saucepan, empty soup. Drain green beans, reserving liquid. Measure green bean liquid in soup can; add enough water to measure 2 soup cans. Gradually stir into soup; add rice and onion salt. Bring to boil; reduce heat. Cover; cook 20 minutes or until rice is done. Stir occasionally. Add sausage and beans; heat. Makes about 6 cups.

A PORK CHOP BY ANY NAME OTHER THAN "CENTER-CUT"
COSTS LESS: Rib, blade, arm, and loin end pork chops are every bit as delicious and nutritious as center-cut—and you'll like the change.

meatless wonders

Step right up folks and taste some amazing main dishes featuring eggs, cheese, and fish. They contain the same high quality protein as meat, but usually cost less. What's more, they are exceptionally delicious and satisfying, as the following recipes demonstrate.

RICE SOUFFLÉ

6 eggs, separated
¼ cup chopped onion
2 teaspoons curry powder
2 tablespoons butter or
  margarine

1 can (10¾ ounces)
  condensed cream of
  mushroom soup
1 cup shredded sharp
  process cheese
1½ cups cooked rice

Beat egg yolks until thick and lemon-colored. In saucepan, cook onion with curry in butter until tender. Blend in soup and cheese; heat slowly until cheese melts. Stir occasionally. Remove from heat; stir yolks into hot soup mixture. Stir in rice. In large bowl, using clean egg beater, beat egg whites until stiff; fold in soup mixture. Pour into an ungreased 2-quart casserole. Bake at 300°F. for 1 hour to 1 hour 15 minutes or until soufflé is golden brown. Serve immediately. Makes 4 to 6 servings.

SPANISH EGGS

½ cup chopped onion
¼ cup chopped green
  pepper
1 medium clove garlic,
  minced
1 tablespoon chili powder
2 tablespoons butter or
  margarine

1 can (10¾ ounces)
  condensed tomato soup
⅓ cup water
¼ cup sliced ripe olives
8 eggs
Salt
Pepper
Shredded Cheddar
  cheese

In saucepan, cook onion and green pepper with garlic and chili in butter until tender. Stir in soup, water, and olives. Cook over low heat 15 minutes; stir occasionally. Pour half of soup mixture into a 2-quart shallow baking dish (12x8x2″); break eggs into sauce. Spoon remaining soup mixture over eggs. Salt and pepper to taste. Bake eggs at 350°F. for 10 to 15 minutes or until set. Garnish with cheese; serve with tortillas. Makes 4 servings.

PUFFY OMELET with CHEESE SAUCE

Omelet:
6 eggs, separated
⅓ cup milk

Dash pepper
3 tablespoons butter or
  margarine

Sauce:
1 can (10¾ ounces)
  condensed cream of
  mushroom soup
½ cup milk
1 cup shredded Swiss
  cheese

1 package (10 ounces)
  frozen asparagus
  spears, cooked and
  drained

To make omelet: Beat egg yolks until thick and lemon-colored; mix in milk and pepper. Using clean egg beater, beat egg whites until stiff but not dry; fold in yolk mixture. Heat butter in oven-proof skillet; pour in eggs. Cook over low heat about 5 minutes or until lightly browned on bottom. Bake at 350°F. for 10 minutes or until top springs back when pressed with finger.
To make sauce: In saucepan, blend soup and milk; add cheese. Heat until cheese melts. Stir occasionally.
Transfer omelet to heated platter. Make a shallow cut down center; top with asparagus. Fold in half. Serve with sauce; sprinkle with paprika. Makes 4 servings.

GARDEN SKILLET

2 cups diced zucchini
½ cup chopped onion
½ teaspoon basil leaves,
  crushed
2 tablespoons butter or
  margarine
1 can (11 ounces)
  condensed Cheddar
  cheese soup

3 cups cooked elbow
  macaroni
2 cups shredded sharp
  Cheddar cheese
1 can (16 ounces)
  tomatoes, chopped and
  well-drained
½ teaspoon prepared
  mustard

In skillet, cook zucchini and onion with basil in butter until tender. Add remaining ingredients. Heat until cheese melts; stir occasionally. Makes about 5½ cups.

BIG BEAN BONANZA

1 can (16 ounces)
    tomatoes, chopped
1 cup sliced onion
1 medium clove garlic,
    minced
1 tablespoon chili powder
2 tablespoons butter or
    margarine
1 can (11½ ounces)
    condensed green pea
    soup

1 can (about 16 ounces)
    lima beans, drained
1 can (15½ ounces) kidney
    beans, undrained
1 can (8½ ounces) butter
    beans, drained
4 slices (about 4 ounces)
    mild process cheese,
    cut in half diagonally

In skillet, simmer tomatoes and onion with garlic and chili
in butter about 15 minutes or until tender. Stir in soup. Add
remaining ingredients except cheese. Heat; stir occasionally. Top with cheese. Cover; heat until cheese melts.
Makes about 5½ cups.

STUFFED FLOUNDER ROLL-UPS

2 packages (10 ounces
    each) frozen broccoli
    spears, cooked and
    drained or 4 medium
    cooked carrots, cut in
    thin sticks
8 fillets of flounder
    (2 pounds)
1 can (10¾ ounces)
    condensed cream of
    celery soup
¼ cup mayonnaise
1 tablespoon lemon juice

Divide broccoli among fillets; roll up. Secure with toothpicks. Arrange in 2-quart shallow baking dish (12x8x2″).
Bake at 350°F. for 20 minutes. Meanwhile, combine remaining ingredients; pour over fish, stirring into liquid
around fish. Bake 15 minutes more or until done. Stir sauce
before serving. Makes 6 to 8 servings.

PATIO TUNA SALAD

1 can (10¾ ounces)
    condensed cream of
    shrimp soup
2 cups cooked elbow
    macaroni
1 can (about 7 ounces)
    tuna, drained and flaked
½ cup diced green pepper
2 tablespoons sliced
    stuffed olives
1 tablespoon finely
    chopped onion
1 tablespoon lemon juice
Dash pepper

In bowl, combine ingredients; chill. Serve on crisp salad greens. Makes about 4 cups.

TUNA CLAM TEMPTER

1 can (19 ounces) chunky
    clam chowder soup
1 can (about 7 ounces)
    tuna, drained and flaked
½ cup cooked whole
    kernel corn
⅛ teaspoon hot pepper
    sauce
1 tablespoon cornstarch
2 tablespoons water

In saucepan, combine soup, tuna, corn, and hot pepper sauce. Blend cornstarch and water until smooth; add to soup mixture. Heat, stirring until thickened. Makes about 3½ cups.

TUNA NOODLE PATTIES

1 can (10¾ ounces) condensed cream of celery soup
2 cans (about 7 ounces each) tuna, drained and flaked
1 cup crushed uncooked fine noodles
½ cup finely chopped celery
2 tablespoons chopped pimiento
¼ cup fine dry bread crumbs
2 tablespoons butter or margarine
¼ cup milk
2 tablespoons chopped parsley
1 tablespoon lemon juice

In bowl, combine ¼ cup soup, tuna, noodles, celery, and pimiento. Shape into 6 patties; coat with bread crumbs. In skillet, brown patties in butter (add more butter if necessary). Meanwhile, in saucepan, combine remaining soup, milk, parsley, and lemon. Heat; stir occasionally. Serve with patties. Makes 6 servings.

SWISS FONDUE

1 can (11 ounces) condensed Cheddar cheese soup
1 package (8 ounces) rectangular slices natural Swiss cheese, cut or torn in pieces
¼ teaspoon prepared mustard
¼ teaspoon Worcestershire
¼ teaspoon hot pepper sauce
French or Italian bread cubes

In saucepan, combine soup, cheese, mustard, Worcestershire, and pepper sauce. Heat until cheese melts. Stir occasionally. Spear bread with fork or toothpick and dip into hot cheese. Makes about 2 cups.

SAVE-ORY SCRAMBLE: *When the price difference between any two sizes of eggs is less than 7 cents, the larger eggs are a better buy than the smaller.*

PLAIN AND FANCY: *What shape is your pasta shelf in? If the good old standbys—elbow macaroni, spaghetti, and noodles–are the extent of your stock, start thinking fancy.*

Unusually shaped pasta may cost slightly more, but it is still one of the least expensive ways to make an otherwise ho-hum meal exciting.

BEFORE-AND-AFTER-THOUGHTS: *Turn oven on AFTER changing rack positions. Turn oven, broiler, and burners off BEFORE removing food. Less energy escapes this way. Less money too.*

LASAGNA MARINARA

⅓ cup very finely chopped onion
¼ teaspoon basil leaves, crushed
⅛ teaspoon thyme leaves, crushed
1 small clove garlic, minced
2 tablespoons salad or olive oil
1 can (10¾ ounces) condensed tomato soup
1 can (about 6 ounces) tomato paste
1½ soup cans water
2 tablespoons grated Parmesan cheese
1 teaspoon salt
1 small bay leaf
9 lasagna noodles (about ½ pound), cooked and drained
2 cups ricotta cheese
1½ cups shredded Mozzarella cheese

In saucepan, cook onion with basil, thyme, and garlic in oil until tender. Blend in soup, tomato paste, water, Parmesan cheese, salt, and bay leaf. Bring to boil; reduce heat. Simmer 30 minutes; stir occasionally. Remove bay leaf. In 2-quart shallow baking dish (12x8x2"), starting with sauce, arrange 3 alternate layers of noodles, ricotta cheese, sauce, and Mozzarella cheese. Sprinkle with additional Parmesan cheese. Bake at 350°F. for 45 minutes or until hot. Let stand 15 minutes before serving. Makes 4 to 6 servings.

POPEYE EGGS 'n' NOODLE BAKE

1 can (10¾ ounces)
    condensed cream of
    mushroom soup
¾ cup water
3 tablespoons soy sauce
⅛ teaspoon ground
    ginger
6 hard-cooked eggs
2 cups cooked noodles
1 package (10 ounces)
    frozen chopped
    spinach, cooked and
    drained
2 slices tomato, cut in half

In 1½-quart casserole, combine soup, water, soy, and ginger. Chop 5 eggs; slice 1 egg and reserve for garnish. Add chopped eggs, noodles, and spinach to soup mixture. Bake at 400°F. for 25 minutes or until hot; stir. Garnish with tomato and reserved sliced egg. Serve with additional soy sauce. Makes about 5 cups.

SAUCY SWEDISH FISH

1 cup carrots sliced
    diagonally
½ cup sliced onion
½ teaspoon dill weed,
    crushed
2 tablespoons butter or
    margarine

1 can (10¾ ounces)
    condensed cream of
    celery soup
1 pound fillets of white
    fish, cut in 2-inch pieces

In skillet, cook carrots and onion with dill in butter until *just* tender. Add soup and fish. Cover; cook over low heat 10 minutes or until done. Stir occasionally. Makes 4 servings.

NEW ENGLAND SCRAMBLE

½ cup chopped green
   pepper
¼ cup chopped onion
2 tablespoons butter or
   margarine

1 can (10¾ ounces)
   condensed New
   England clam chowder
8 eggs, slightly beaten
Dash pepper

In 10" skillet, cook green pepper and onion in butter until tender. In bowl, stir soup until smooth; gradually blend in eggs and pepper. Pour into skillet. Cook over low heat; do not stir. As mixture begins to set around edges, gently lift cooked portions with large turner so that thin, uncooked portion can flow to the bottom. Continue gently lifting cooked portions until eggs are completely set, but still moist (about 8 minutes). Makes 4 servings.

TUNA WAIKIKI

1 can (10¾ ounces)
   condensed cream of
   mushroom soup
½ cup milk
2 cans (about 7 ounces
   each) tuna, drained and
   flaked
1 cup drained canned
   pineapple chunks
¼ cup chopped toasted
   almonds

2 tablespoons finely
   chopped onion
1 teaspoon soy sauce
4 slices French or Italian
   bread
2 tablespoons melted
   butter or margarine
¼ teaspoon dried parsley
   flakes, crushed

In 1½-quart shallow baking dish (10x6x2"), combine soup, milk, tuna, pineapple, almonds, onion, and soy; top with bread. Brush bread with butter; sprinkle with parsley. Bake at 400°F. for 30 minutes or until hot. Makes about 5 cups.

Yankee Chili—recipe page 95

CHEESY SPINACH 'n' RICE BAKE

½ cup chopped onion
2 tablespoons butter or
  margarine
1 can (10¾ ounces)
  condensed cream of
  mushroom soup
2 cups cooked rice
2 cups shredded sharp
  Cheddar cheese
1 package (10 ounces)
  frozen chopped
  spinach, cooked and
  well-drained
4 eggs, slightly beaten
¼ teaspoon
  Worcestershire
⅛ teaspoon thyme leaves,
  crushed

In saucepan, cook onion in butter until tender. Stir in remaining ingredients. Spoon mixture into 1½-quart shallow baking dish (10x6x2"). Bake at 375°F. for 45 minutes or until set. Makes about 6 cups.

TIME OFF: *Give your refrigerator and freezer a break. If you have a choice, locate them away from heating equipment and direct sunlight so they don't have to work so hard.*

Garden Skillet—recipe page 60

TUNA TOMATO-WICH

1 small green pepper, cut in strips
1 tablespoon butter or margarine
1 can (10¾ ounces) condensed golden mushroom soup
⅓ cup water
1 can (about 7 ounces) tuna, drained and flaked
1 medium tomato, cut in wedges
Toast
Sliced onion

In skillet, cook green pepper in butter until tender. Add soup, water, and tuna. Heat; stir occasionally. Add tomato wedges; heat. Serve on toast. Garnish with onion. Makes about 3 cups.

ALL-IN-ONE TUNA CASSEROLE

1 can (10¾ ounces) condensed cream of onion soup
½ cup sour cream
½ cup milk
2 cups cooked elbow macaroni
1 package (9 ounces) frozen cut green beans, cooked and drained
1 can (about 7 ounces) tuna, drained and flaked
¼ cup diced pimiento
1 tablespoon lemon juice
⅛ teaspoon thyme leaves, crushed
Sliced hard-cooked eggs
Parsley

In 1½-quart casserole, stir soup and sour cream; gradually add milk and remaining ingredients except eggs and parsley. Bake at 400°F. for 30 minutes or until hot; stir. Garnish with eggs and parsley. Makes about 5 cups.

SING A SONG OF SALMON: But stay in tune with your budget. Color is the clue—the redder the salmon the higher the price. From reddest to pinkest are Sockeye, King, Silver, Pink, and Chum.

Look at the label and buy right: Pink is ideal for loaves and patties since it breaks into flakes. The deeper reds are good for salads and casseroles since these varieties break into large chunks.

POMPEII TUNA

½ cup diagonally sliced
  celery
1 medium clove garlic,
  minced
½ teaspoon oregano
  leaves, crushed
2 tablespoons butter or
  margarine
1 can (11 ounces)
  condensed Cheddar
  cheese soup

½ cup water
1 can (about 7 ounces)
  tuna, drained and flaked
2 cups cooked spaghetti
1 cup cooked cut green
  beans
½ cup chopped canned
  tomatoes

In saucepan, cook celery with garlic and oregano in butter
until tender. Add remaining ingredients. Heat; stir occasionally. Makes about 5 cups.

TUNA TETRAZZINI

2 tablespoons chopped
  onion
1 tablespoon butter or
  margarine
1 can (10¾ ounces)
  condensed cream of
  mushroom soup
½ cup water
½ cup shredded sharp
  Cheddar cheese
1 can (about 7 ounces)
  tuna, drained and flaked
2 tablespoons diced
  pimiento
1 tablespoon chopped
  parsley
2 cups cooked spaghetti

In saucepan, cook onion in butter until tender. Blend in
soup, water, and cheese. Cook over low heat until cheese
melts; stir occasionally. Add tuna, pimiento, parsley, and
spaghetti. Heat; stir occasionally. Makes about 3½ cups.

STUFFED SHELLS NEAPOLITAN

1 can (10¾ ounces)
  condensed cream of
  celery soup
½ teaspoon lemon juice
¼ teaspoon oregano
  leaves, crushed
1 package (10 ounces)
  frozen chopped
  broccoli, cooked and
  well-drained

½ cup drained chopped
  canned tomatoes
1 can (about 7 ounces)
  tuna, drained and flaked
12 jumbo shells macaroni,
  cooked and drained
½ cup shredded Cheddar
  cheese

Combine soup, lemon juice, oregano, broccoli, tomatoes, and tuna. Stuff about ¼ cup mixture into each shell. In 1½-quart shallow baking dish (10 × 6 × 2"), arrange stuffed shells. Bake at 400°F. for 20 minutes or until hot. Sprinkle with cheese; bake 5 minutes more or until cheese melts. Garnish with parsley if desired. Makes 4 servings.

CLAM SPAGHETTI SUPPER

¼ cup chopped onion
1 small clove garlic,
  minced
1 tablespoon butter or
  margarine
1 can (19 ounces) chunky
  clam chowder soup

½ cup uncooked thin
  spaghetti broken in
  pieces
½ cup chopped parsley

In saucepan, cook onion with garlic in butter until tender. Add remaining ingredients. Cover; cook over low heat 20 minutes or until spaghetti is done. Stir often. Makes about 2 cups.

RIPE, RIPER, RIPEST: Ripen tomatoes, avocados, melons, peaches, pears, and plums at room temperature out of direct sunlight. Then refrigerate until ready to use.

TAKE A CAN OF TUNA: *But which one? So many kinds crowd the market shelves.*

A word to the pennywise: Tuna is priced by **type**—*white is costlier than light. And by* **pack**—*according to the size of the pieces. Fancy-or solid-pack tuna is most expensive, so save it for something special. Chunk tuna comes next—a natural for casseroles since the pieces hold their shape. Flaked tuna makes an ideal sandwich filling because the fish is already in small pieces.*

Choose the tuna that best fits your needs, and remember—all tuna is created nutritionally equal, no matter what the price.

TUNA LOAF WITH HORSERADISH SAUCE

1 can (10¾ ounces)
  condensed tomato soup
2 cans (about 7 ounces
  each) tuna, drained and
  flaked
1 cup small bread cubes
2 eggs, slightly beaten

2 tablespoons chopped
  parsley
2 teaspoons lemon juice
2 tablespoons water
1 tablespoon prepared
  horseradish
⅛ teaspoon basil leaves,
  crushed

Mix *thoroughly* ½ cup soup, tuna, bread cubes, eggs, parsley, and lemon juice. Spread evenly in well-greased loaf pan (8x4x3″). Bake at 400°F. for 40 minutes. Loosen edges; unmold. Meanwhile, combine remaining soup, water, horseradish, and basil. Heat; stir occasionally. Serve with loaf. Makes 6 servings.

TOMATO-MUSHROOM RABBIT

1 can (about 2 ounces)
  sliced mushrooms,
  drained
2 tablespoons chopped
  onion
2 tablespoons butter or
  margarine

1 can (11 ounces)
  condensed Cheddar
  cheese soup
¼ teaspoon prepared
  mustard
¼ cup milk
Toast
Tomato slices

In saucepan, brown mushrooms and cook onion in butter until tender. Blend in soup and mustard; gradually add milk. Heat; stir occasionally. Top toast with tomato slices; pour sauce over all. Makes about 1½ cups.

YOUR TURN TO WASH? *Soiled dishes needn't take your hot water bill out of sight. Simply avoid running the hot water for long periods.*

Use a pan of sudsy hot water to wash, a pan of plain hot water to rinse . . . glassware first, eating utensils next, followed by plates, and finally, pots and pans.

TUNA A LA KING

½ cup sliced celery
2 tablespoons chopped onion
1 tablespoon butter or margarine
1 can (10¾ ounces) condensed cream of mushroom soup

⅓ cup milk
1 can (about 7 ounces) tuna, drained and flaked
2 tablespoons chopped pimiento
Toast or biscuits

In saucepan, cook celery and onion in butter until tender. Stir in soup, milk, tuna, and pimiento. Heat; stir occasionally. Serve over toast. Garnish with chopped parsley if desired. Makes about 2½ cups.

TUNA NOODLE COMBO

1 can (10¾ ounces) condensed cream of celery soup
½ cup sour cream
½ cup milk
1 can (about 7 ounces) tuna, drained and flaked
2 tablespoons chopped parsley

2 tablespoons chopped pimiento
¼ teaspoon salt
Generous dash pepper
2 cups cooked noodles
2 tablespoons buttered bread crumbs

Blend soup and sour cream; stir in milk. Add tuna, parsley, pimiento, seasonings, and noodles. Pour into 1½-quart casserole. Bake at 400°F. for 25 minutes or until hot; stir. Top with bread crumbs. Bake 5 minutes more. Makes about 4 cups.

TUNA SALAD LAMAZE

1 can (10¾ ounces)
condensed tomato soup
1 cup mayonnaise
¼ cup sweet pickle relish
1 tablespoon lemon juice
½ teaspoon grated onion
½ teaspoon prepared
mustard

2 cups cubed cooked
potatoes
1 package (9 ounces)
frozen cut green beans,
cooked and drained
1 can (about 7 ounces)
tuna, drained and flaked

Combine soup, mayonnaise, relish, lemon, onion, and
mustard. Mix 1 cup soup mixture with potatoes and beans.
Chill 1 hour or more. Arrange potato mixture on crisp salad
greens; top with tuna. Serve with remaining dressing.
Makes 4 servings.

EASY OVEN FILLETS

1 pound fillets of white fish
(haddock, flounder, or
other white fish)
1 can (about 16 ounces)
small whole white
potatoes, drained

1 can (10¾ ounces)
condensed cream of
celery soup
2 tablespoons chopped
parsley
Paprika

Arrange fish and potatoes in single layer in 2-quart shallow
baking dish (12x8x2″). Bake at 350°F. for 15 minutes. Pour
soup over, stirring into liquid around fish. Bake 10 minutes
more or until done. Stir sauce before serving. Sprinkle with
parsley and paprika if desired. Makes 3 servings.

*CUPBOARD, CUPBOARD ON THE WALL: Who's the thriftiest of
all? You are, if you can afford the storage space for staples such
as canned goods when they're on special. If not, consider a
do-it-yourself shelf project in some cool, dry spot.*

pot luck

Ahh, the joys of a one-pot supper—simplicity in preparation and cleanup, old-fashioned flavors, tantalizing smells. Dish out some down-home goodness tonight with one of the following stews, roasts, or meal-in-a-bowl soups.

BEEF 'n' BEANS

2 frankfurters, sliced
1 tablespoon butter or
　margarine
1 can (19 ounces) chunky
　beef soup
1 can (16 ounces) pork &
　beans with tomato sauce

2 teaspoons prepared
　mustard
½ teaspoon prepared
　horseradish

In saucepan, brown frankfurters in butter. Add remaining ingredients. Heat; stir occasionally. Makes about 4 cups.

SPANISH CHICKEN

2 pounds chicken parts
2 tablespoons shortening
1 can (10¾ ounces)
　condensed chicken
　broth
½ cup water
2 medium cloves garlic,
　minced

1 teaspoon salt
½ cup chopped onion
⅔ cup raw regular rice
1 package (10 ounces)
　frozen peas
1 cup cut-up canned
　tomatoes

In skillet, slowly brown chicken in shortening (about 30 minutes); pour off fat. Remove chicken. Stir in remaining ingredients except peas and tomatoes; top with chicken. Cover; cook over low heat 15 minutes. Stir occasionally. Add peas and tomatoes. Cook 10 minutes more or until done. Makes 4 servings.

HAM AND PEA TETRAZZINI

1½ cups cooked ham cut
　in strips
1 small clove garlic,
　minced
2 tablespoons butter or
　margarine
1 can (10¾ ounces)
　condensed cream of
　chicken soup

¾ cup milk
1 cup shredded Swiss
　cheese
1 package (10 ounces)
　frozen peas, cooked
　and drained
2 cups cooked spaghetti

In saucepan, brown ham with garlic in butter. Add soup, milk, and cheese. Heat until cheese melts; stir occasionally. Add peas and spaghetti; heat. Makes about 5½ cups.

BRUNSWICK STEW

2 slices bacon
2 pounds chicken parts
1 can (10¾ ounces)
   condensed tomato soup
⅓ cup water
½ cup sliced onion
1 teaspoon
   Worcestershire
1 medium clove garlic,
   minced
½ teaspoon salt
Dash pepper
1 package (10 ounces)
   frozen whole okra
1 package (10 ounces)
   frozen succotash

In large heavy pan, cook bacon until crisp; remove and crumble. Pour off all but 2 tablespoons drippings. Brown chicken in drippings. Stir in soup, water, onion, Worcestershire, garlic, salt, and pepper. Cover; cook over low heat 15 minutes. Add vegetables. Cook 30 minutes more or until done. Stir occasionally. Spoon off fat. Garnish with bacon. Makes 4 servings.

PROVINCIAL HAM POTAGE

1½ cups diced cooked
   ham
½ cup chopped onion
¼ teaspoon dried dill
   weed, crushed
2 tablespoons butter or
   margarine
1 can (10¾ ounces)
   condensed cream of
   celery soup

1 can (10¾ ounces)
   condensed cream of
   chicken soup
1 soup can milk
1 soup can water
1 package (9 ounces)
   French style green
   beans, cooked and
   drained
1 cup sliced cooked
   carrots

In saucepan, brown ham and cook onion with dill in butter until tender. Stir in soups; gradually blend in milk and water. Add remaining ingredients. Heat; stir occasionally. Makes about 7½ cups.

CALICO STEW

½ pound bulk sausage
2 pounds chicken parts
1 can (10¾ ounces) condensed tomato soup
¼ cup water

1 teaspoon oregano leaves, crushed
¼ teaspoon paprika
4 ears frozen corn on the cob, thawed and cut in half

In large heavy pan, brown sausage; stir to separate meat. Remove; drain. Brown chicken in drippings; pour off fat. Add sausage and remaining ingredients except corn. Cover; cook over low heat 25 minutes. Stir occasionally. Add corn; cook 20 minutes more or until done. Makes 4 servings.

NEW MATH: *Cook double and subtract from your utility bill. When you make twice as much spaghetti sauce, Stroganoff, stew, even two casseroles—and freeze part for another meal—you use less heat, and save, save, save. Less work for the chef, too.*

COUNTY FAIR CHICKEN

3 pounds chicken parts
2 tablespoons shortening
2 cans (10¾ ounces each) condensed cream of mushroom soup
1½ soup cans water
¼ teaspoon thyme leaves, crushed

¼ teaspoon salt
Generous dash pepper
3 cups uncooked medium noodles
1 package (9 ounces) frozen cut green beans

In large heavy pan, brown chicken in shortening; pour off fat. Add soup, water, and seasonings. Cover; cook over low heat 30 minutes. Add noodles and green beans. Cook 20 minutes more or until done. Stir occasionally. Makes 6 servings.

BUTTERMILK CHUCK STEW

3½-pound boneless chuck
   roast (about 2-inch
   thick)
2 tablespoons shortening
2 cans (10¾ ounces each)
   condensed cream of
   mushroom soup
1½ cups buttermilk
¾ cup water
1 cup chopped onion

¼ teaspoon ground
   nutmeg
⅛ teaspoon pepper
4 medium carrots (about
   ½ pound), cut in 1½-inch
   pieces
1 small head cauliflower
   (about 1 pound),
   separated into
   flowerets

Trim fat from meat; cut in 1½-inch cubes. In large heavy
oven-proof pan, brown meat in shortening; pour off fat.
Stir in soup, buttermilk, water, onion, nutmeg, and pepper.
Cover; bake at 350°F. for 1 hour 30 minutes. Add carrots;
stir mixture. Bake 30 minutes more. Arrange cauliflower on
top of stew; bake 30 minutes more or until done. Garnish
with parsley if desired. Makes about 10 cups.

IRISH CHUCK ROAST

3½-pound boneless chuck
   roast (about 2-inch
   thick)
2 tablespoons shortening
2 cans (10¾ ounces each)
   condensed golden
   mushroom soup
½ cup chopped canned
   tomatoes
1 tablespoon prepared
   horseradish
½ teaspoon celery seed
6 small potatoes (about
   1½ pounds), cut in half
1 medium head cabbage,
   cut in 6 wedges

In large heavy pan, brown meat in shortening; pour off fat.
Add soup, tomatoes, horseradish, and celery seed. Cover;
cook over low heat 2 hours. Add potatoes; place cabbage
on top. Cook 1 hour more or until done. Stir occasionally.
Spoon off fat; thicken sauce if desired. Makes 6 servings.

PIQUANT BEEF POT

2 cans (10¾ ounces each)
   condensed cream of
   potato soup
1 soup can milk
½ soup can water
2 cups cubed cooked beef
½ cup shredded Cheddar
   cheese

1 package (10 ounces)
   frozen mixed
   vegetables, cooked and
   drained
2 tablespoons chopped
   parsley
2 teaspoons prepared
   horseradish

In saucepan, combine ingredients. Heat; stir occasionally.
Makes about 7 cups.

LANCASTER COUNTY MEATBALLS

1 pound ground beef
1 egg, slightly beaten
¼ cup fine dry bread
   crumbs
2 tablespoons finely
   chopped onion
⅛ teaspoon salt
⅛ teaspoon pepper

2 tablespoons shortening
1 cup thinly sliced carrots
2 cans (10½ ounces each)
   condensed beef broth
2 soup cans water
1 small bay leaf
1½ cups medium noodles,
   broken in pieces

Mix *thoroughly* beef, egg, bread crumbs, onion, salt, and
pepper; shape into 24 meatballs. In large heavy pan, brown
meatballs in shortening; pour off fat. Add remaining ingredients. Bring to boil; reduce heat. Simmer 10 minutes or
until noodles are done. Stir occasionally. Remove bay leaf.
Garnish with sour cream if desired. Makes about 7 cups.

MINUTEMAN SKILLET

½ cup sliced celery
2 tablespoons butter or
   margarine
1 can (10¾ ounces)
   condensed cream of
   mushroom soup
2 cups cooked rice

1½ cups cubed cooked
   chicken
1 can (about 8 ounces)
   sliced carrots,
   undrained
Grated Parmesan cheese

In skillet, cook celery in butter until tender. Add soup, rice,
chicken, and carrots. Heat; stir occasionally. Serve with
cheese. Makes about 4 cups.

QUICK CHICKEN CORN CHOWDER

½ cup chopped onion
¼ teaspoon poultry
　seasoning
⅛ teaspoon pepper
2 tablespoons butter or
　margarine
1 can (10¾ ounces)
　condensed cream of
　chicken soup

1 can (10¾ ounces)
　condensed cream of
　potato soup
1 soup can milk
1 soup can water
1½ cups diced cooked
　chicken
1 can (about 8 ounces)
　cream style corn

In large saucepan, cook onion with seasonings in butter until tender. Add soups; gradually stir in milk and water. Add chicken and corn. Heat; stir occasionally. Garnish with chopped parsley if desired. Makes about 7 cups.

HEARTY TRIPLE TREAT

1 can (19 ounces) chunky
　chicken with rice soup
1 can (19 ounces) chunky
　vegetable soup

1 can (16 ounces) home
　style beans

In saucepan, combine ingredients. Heat; stir occasionally. Makes about 6 cups.

SPICEBOX STEW

1½ pounds beef cubes
　(1½ inch)
2 tablespoons shortening
2 cans (10¾ ounces each)
　condensed tomato soup
½ cup water
½ cup Burgundy or other
　dry red wine
1 small bay leaf

¼ teaspoon thyme leaves,
　crushed
3 medium potatoes (about
　1 pound), quartered
8 small whole white
　onions (½ pound)
1 package (10 ounces)
　frozen peas

In large heavy pan, brown beef in shortening; pour off fat. Add soup, water, Burgundy, bay leaf, and thyme. Cover; cook over low heat 1 hour 30 minutes. Add potatoes and onions. Cook 45 minutes; add peas. Cook 15 minutes more or until done. Stir occasionally. Remove bay leaf. Makes about 8 cups.

__THE CHEESE STANDS ALONE:__ And for good reason. Store strong-flavored cheeses in tightly covered jars in the refrigerator to prevent their odor from spreading to other foods.

MEATBALL STEW

1 pound ground beef
1 egg, slightly beaten
½ cup small bread cubes
¾ cup finely chopped onion
½ teaspoon salt
2 tablespoons shortening
1 can (10½ ounces) condensed beef broth
1 can (10¾ ounces) condensed tomato soup

⅛ teaspoon thyme leaves, crushed
1 can (about 16 ounces) small whole white potatoes, drained and cut up
1 can (about 8 ounces) peas, undrained

Mix *thoroughly* beef, egg, bread cubes, ¼ cup onion, and salt. Shape firmly into 36 meatballs. In large heavy pan, brown meatballs in shortening; pour off fat. Add remaining ingredients. Heat; stir occasionally. Makes about 6½ cups.

PORK LOIN-TO-PERFECTION

3 to 4-pound pork loin rib roast
2 tablespoons shortening
1 can (10¾ ounces) condensed golden mushroom soup
½ cup water
½ cup chopped onion
1 tablespoon paprika

1 medium bay leaf
½ teaspoon salt
Dash pepper
6 medium carrots, cut in 2-inch pieces
4 medium potatoes, cut in half

In large heavy pan, brown meat in shortening; pour off fat. Add soup, water, onion, and seasonings. Cover; cook over low heat 1 hour 15 minutes. Stir occasionally. Add carrots and potatoes. Cook 1 hour more or until done. Remove bay leaf. Thicken sauce if desired. Makes 4 to 6 servings.

DUTCH CHOWDER 'n' DUMPLINGS

1½ cups cooked pork cut
  in strips
¼ cup chopped onion
2 tablespoons butter or
  margarine
2 cans (11¼ ounces each)
  condensed green pea
  soup
1½ soup cans water
1 package (10 ounces)
  frozen mixed
  vegetables, cooked
  and drained
¼ teaspoon ground
  nutmeg
Generous dash salt
½ cup biscuit mix
2 teaspoons chopped
  parsley
3 tablespoons milk

In saucepan, brown pork and cook onion in butter until tender. Add soup; gradually blend in water. Add vegetables, nutmeg, and salt. Bring to boil. Meanwhile, combine biscuit mix, parsley, and milk; drop by teaspoonsful into simmering soup. Cook 5 minutes. Cover; cook 5 minutes more or until done. Makes about 6½ cups.

ORIENTAL BEEF 'n' VEGETABLES

½ pound ground beef
½ cup sliced onion
2 cans (19 ounces each)
  chunky vegetable soup
1 can (16 ounces) Chinese
  vegetables, drained

1 tablespoon soy sauce
1 tablespoon cornstarch
Chinese noodles or
  cooked rice

In saucepan, brown beef and cook onion until tender (use shortening if necessary). Stir to separate meat; pour off fat. Add remaining ingredients except noodles. Cook, stirring until thickened. Serve over Chinese noodles with additional soy. Makes about 6 cups.

PORK LOIN with CARAWAY GRAVY

3-pound boneless rolled
  loin of pork
Generous dash pepper
1 can (11 ounces)
  condensed Cheddar
  cheese soup
1 tablespoon vinegar
1 teaspoon brown sugar
½ teaspoon caraway seed

4 medium carrots (about
  ½ pound), quartered
1 medium head cabbage,
  cut in 4 wedges
¼ cup water
2 tablespoons flour

In roasting pan (13x9x2″), place meat fat-side up. Season
with pepper. Roast at 325°F. for 1 hour. Pour off all but 2
tablespoons drippings; stir in soup, vinegar, sugar, and
caraway. Arrange carrots around meat; top with cabbage.
Cover with foil. Roast 2 hours more or until done (total
roasting time takes 35 to 40 minutes per pound or 170°F. on
meat thermometer). Remove meat and vegetables to serving platter; keep warm. Gradually blend water into flour
until smooth. On top of range, in roasting pan, slowly stir
flour mixture into sauce. Cook, stirring until thickened.
Serve with roast. Makes 6 to 8 servings.

MEXICAN HASH

1 can (about 16 ounces)
  prepared tamales
2 cans (19 ounces each)
  chunky beef soup

½ cup sliced ripe olives
1 teaspoon chili powder
1 cup shredded sharp
  Cheddar cheese

Remove wrappings from tamales; cut in half. In saucepan,
combine tamales, soup, olives, and chili. Heat; stir occasionally. Garnish with cheese. Makes about 6 cups.

POTS, PANS, AND PEARLS OF WISDOM: *Did you know that a
tight-fitting lid on saucepans and skillets can save you money?
With well-covered utensils, less heat escapes into the air, so you
can use lower heat settings and shorter cooking times.*

*Check the bottoms of your pans. If they are flat, they make
firmer contact with surface elements, distributing heat more
evenly and efficiently.*

CHEESY RAVIOLIOS SOUP

¼ pound hot Italian
   sausage, cut in 1-inch
   pieces
¼ cup chopped onion
1 can (11 ounces)
   Cheddar cheese soup
1 soup can water

1 can (15 ounces) beef
   raviolios in meat sauce
1 can (about 16 ounces)
   cut green beans,
   drained
2 tablespoons diced
   pimiento

In saucepan, cook sausage until done. Add onion; cook
until tender. Pour off fat. Stir in soup; gradually add remaining ingredients. Heat; stir occasionally. Makes about
5½ cups.

CAPE COD KETTLE

1 can (10½ ounces)
   condensed oyster stew
1 can (10¾ ounces)
   condensed cream of
   potato soup
2 soup cans milk
1 can (about 7 ounces)
   salmon or tuna, drained
   and flaked

1 can (about 8 ounces)
   whole kernel corn,
   undrained
1 tablespoon chopped
   parsley

In saucepan, combine ingredients. Heat; stir occasionally.
Makes about 6½ cups.

SAUSAGE SUPPER SOUP

1 package (8 ounces)
   brown 'n serve sausage
   links, sliced
1 can (10¾ ounces)
   condensed cream of
   chicken soup
1 soup can water

1 package (10 ounces)
   frozen mixed
   vegetables, cooked
   and drained
1 cup cubed zucchini
¼ teaspoon thyme leaves,
   crushed

In saucepan, brown sausage; pour off fat. Add remaining
ingredients. Cook 10 minutes or until vegetables are tender; stir occasionally. Makes about 5 cups.

HAMBURGER SOUP OLÉ

½ pound ground beef
¼ teaspoon salt
Generous dash pepper
½ cup chopped onion
1 small green pepper, cut
   in squares
1 large clove garlic,
   minced
¼ teaspoon oregano
   leaves, crushed

1 can (11 ounces)
   condensed Cheddar
   cheese soup
1 can (11¼ ounces)
   condensed chili beef
   soup
1½ soup cans water
1 can (about 8 ounces)
   whole kernel golden
   corn, undrained

Season beef with salt and pepper; shape into 16 meatballs. In large saucepan, brown meatballs and cook onion and green pepper with garlic and oregano until tender (use shortening if necessary). Stir in soups; gradually blend in water. Add corn. Heat; stir occasionally. Makes about 7 cups.

SUNDAY POT ROAST

3 to 4-pound boneless pot
   roast
1 can (10½ ounces)
   condensed beef broth
½ teaspoon salt
¼ teaspoon pepper
¼ teaspoon rosemary
   leaves, crushed
6 small carrots, cut in half
   lengthwise (about ½
   pound)
2 medium yellow turnips,
   quartered (about 1½
   pounds)
8 small whole white
   onions (about ½ pound)

In large heavy pan, brown meat on all sides (use shortening if necessary); pour off fat. Add broth and seasonings. Cover; cook over low heat 2 hours. Add carrots, turnips, and onions. Cook 1 hour more or until done. Stir occasionally. Remove meat and vegetables to heated platter. Spoon off fat; thicken to desired consistency. Makes 6 to 8 servings.

CONFETTI CHICKEN CHOWDER

4 slices bacon
1 can (about 4 ounces)
    sliced mushrooms,
    drained
½ cup chopped onion
⅛ teaspoon thyme leaves,
    crushed
1 can (10¾ ounces)
    condensed cream of
    celery soup
1 can (10½ ounces)
    condensed chicken
    vegetable soup

1 soup can water
1½ cups diced cooked
    chicken
1 can (about 8 ounces)
    whole kernel corn,
    undrained
½ cup chopped canned
    tomatoes
Dash pepper

In saucepan, cook bacon until crisp; remove and crumble. Pour off all but 2 tablespoons drippings. Brown mushrooms and cook onion with thyme in drippings until tender. Add remaining ingredients except bacon. Heat; stir occasionally. Garnish with bacon. Makes about 5½ cups.

PIZZA POTAGE

½ pound ground beef
¼ teaspoon onion salt
2 tablespoons shortening
1 can (10½ ounces)
    condensed old
    fashioned vegetable
    soup
1 can (10¾ ounces)
    condensed tomato soup

1½ soup cans water
1 cup cooked
    spiral-shaped macaroni
2 tablespoons chopped
    parsley
¼ teaspoon oregano
    leaves, crushed
Grated Parmesan cheese

Mix *thoroughly* beef and onion salt; shape into 12 meatballs. In saucepan, brown meatballs in shortening; pour off fat. Add remaining ingredients except cheese. Heat; stir occasionally. Serve with cheese. Makes about 6 cups.

WESTERN CHILI

1 pound ground beef
½ cup chopped green
   pepper
½ cup chopped onion
2 tablespoons chili
   powder
2 cans (11¼ ounces each)
   condensed chili beef
   soup

½ cup water
1 can (16 ounces)
   tomatoes, cut up
1 can (15½ ounces) kidney
   beans, undrained

In large saucepan, brown beef and cook green pepper and onion with chili powder until tender (use shortening if necessary). Stir to separate meat. Add remaining ingredients. Simmer 15 minutes; stir often. Makes about 8 cups.

BEEF BURGUNDY GOULASH

1½ pounds beef cubes
   (1½ inch)
2 tablespoons shortening
2 cans (10½ ounces each)
   condensed onion soup
½ soup can water

½ soup can Burgundy or
   other dry red wine
3 cups uncooked medium
   noodles
1 cup sliced carrots

In large heavy pan, brown beef in shortening; pour off fat. Add soup, water, and Burgundy. Cover; cook over low heat 2 hours. Add noodles and carrots. Cook 20 minutes more or until done. Stir occasionally. Add additional water if necessary. Makes about 6 cups.

BROWN-BAGGING CAN BE BEAUTIFUL: *For business people and scholars of every description, the carried lunch offers a pennywise alternative to the cafeteria line. Here's a perfect niche for leftovers and a good excuse to put your imagination in high gear.*

For starters, pack soup in vacuum containers. Rinse the vacuum bottle with hot water before pouring in hot soup, cold water for cold soup.

Add a sandwich—or a salad—or fruit and cheese.

AUTUMN BEEF STEW

2 pounds beef cubes (1½ inch)
2 tablespoons shortening
2 cans (10¾ ounces each) condensed golden mushroom or cream of mushroom soup
½ cup water
1 tablespoon Worcestershire
6 medium carrots, cut in 2-inch pieces
8 small whole white onions (about ½ pound)
1 package (9 ounces) frozen cut green beans
Cooked noodles

In large heavy pan, brown beef in shortening; pour off fat. Add soup, water, and Worcestershire. Cover; cook over low heat 1 hour 30 minutes. Add carrots and onions. Cook 45 minutes more. Add beans. Cook 15 minutes more or until done. Stir occasionally. Thicken sauce if desired. Serve over noodles. Makes about 7 cups.

OLD-FASHIONED SUPPER SOUP

½ cup chopped onion
1 medium clove garlic, minced
1 teaspoon basil leaves, crushed
2 tablespoons butter or margarine
2 cans (10¾ ounces each) condensed golden mushroom soup
2 soup cans water
1 can (about 16 ounces) stewed tomatoes, cut up
2 cups diced cooked chicken or turkey
1½ cups uncooked medium noodles

In large heavy pan, cook onion and garlic with basil in butter until tender. Stir in soup and water; add remaining ingredients. Bring to boil; reduce heat. Cook 10 minutes or until noodles are done; stir occasionally. Makes about 8 cups.

THE ROAST WITH THE MOST: *When comparing the cost of similar foods, especially meat, consider cost per serving rather than cost per pound or total cost.*

A boneless roast, for instance, is often more economical than a cheaper per-pound cut with bone, simply because you wind up with more servings.

CHUCK STEAK and VEGETABLES

4 medium carrots (about ½ pound), halved lengthwise
2-pound boneless chuck steak (1-inch thick), well trimmed
2 tablespoons shortening

Dash salt
Dash paprika
Dash pepper
1 can (10½ ounces) condensed onion soup
3 medium potatoes (about 1 pound), quartered

Cut carrots into 3-inch pieces. In large heavy pan, brown steak in shortening; pour off fat. Season with salt, paprika, and pepper. Add soup. Cover; cook over low heat 45 minutes. Add carrots and potatoes. Cook 45 minutes more or until done. Stir occasionally. Spoon off fat; thicken sauce if desired. Makes 4 servings.

KENTUCKY CHICKEN CHOWDER

1 cup chopped onion
¼ teaspoon basil leaves, crushed
¼ teaspoon thyme leaves, crushed
2 tablespoons butter or margarine
2 cans (10¾ ounces each) condensed chicken broth

2 cups shredded raw potato
1½ cups cubed cooked chicken
1 package (10 ounces) frozen succotash
1 cup cut-up canned tomatoes
1 soup can water
⅛ teaspoon pepper

In large saucepan, cook onion with basil and thyme in butter until tender. Add remaining ingredients. Bring to boil; reduce heat. Cover; simmer 20 minutes or until vegetables are done. Stir often. Makes about 8 cups.

91

HEARTY BEEF STEW

1½ pounds beef cubes
  (1 inch)
2 tablespoons shortening
1 can (10¾ ounces)
  condensed golden
  mushroom soup

1 medium bay leaf
3 cups frozen stew
  vegetables

In large heavy pan, brown beef in shortening; pour off fat.
Add soup and bay leaf. Cover; simmer 1 hour 30 minutes.
Add stew vegetables. Cook 30 minutes more or until done;
stir occasionally. Makes about 4 cups.

FRANKFURTER CREOLE CHOWDER

1 pound frankfurters, cut
  in ½-inch slices
¼ teaspoon basil or thyme
  leaves, crushed
2 tablespoons butter or
  margarine
1 can (11½ ounces)
  condensed split pea
  with ham soup

1 can (10¾ ounces)
  condensed cream of
  potato soup
½ soup can water
1 cup cut-up canned
  tomatoes
1 can (about 8 ounces)
  whole kernel golden
  corn, undrained

In large saucepan, brown frankfurters with basil in butter.
Add soups; gradually stir in water. Add remaining ingredients. Heat; stir occasionally. Makes about 6 cups.

THE BIG BIRD OF HAPPINESS: When it comes to buying turkey
and chicken, think big and save. The larger the bird, the more
meat and less bone and fat per pound. What's more, leftovers can
be transformed into delicious main dishes like *DEEP DISH TUR-
KEY PIE (page 7).*

Do make sure your oven and refrigerator can hold these
heavyweights, however.

soup mates

**Team up two different soups in a saucepan
and you've got something to cheer about.**

ONE SOUP + SECOND SOUP + LIQUID = SOUP MATE

Simply heat and stir.

BEAN WITH BACON	BEEF	1½ SOUP CANS WATER
BEEF	VEGETABLE BEEF	1½ SOUP CANS WATER
BEEF BROTH	TOMATO	1½ SOUP CANS WATER
CREAM OF CELERY	GREEN PEA	1½ SOUP CANS WATER
CHEDDAR CHEESE	TOMATO BISQUE	2 SOUP CANS WATER
CHICKEN 'N DUMPLINGS	CHICKEN VEGETABLE	1½ SOUP CANS WATER
CHICKEN GUMBO	MANHATTAN STYLE CLAM CHOWDER	1½ SOUP CANS WATER
CHICKEN GUMBO	CHICKEN NOODLE-O'S	1½ SOUP CANS WATER
CHICKEN GUMBO	VEGETABLE	1½ SOUP CANS WATER
CHICKEN NOODLE	CHICKEN & STARS	1½ SOUP CANS WATER
CHICKEN VEGETABLE	GOLDEN VEGETABLE NOODLE-O'S	1½ SOUP CANS WATER
CHILI BEEF	VEGETABLE BEEF	1½ SOUP CANS WATER
GOLDEN MUSHROOM	NOODLES & GROUND BEEF	1½ SOUP CANS WATER
GOLDEN MUSHROOM	STOCKPOT	1½ SOUP CANS WATER
CREAM OF MUSHROOM	CREAM OF SHRIMP	1 SOUP CAN MILK 1 SOUP CAN WATER
NOODLES & GROUND BEEF	TOMATO RICE	1½ SOUP CANS WATER
ONION	STOCKPOT	1½ SOUP CANS WATER
PEPPER POT	VEGETABLE BEEF	1½ SOUP CANS WATER
SPLIT PEA WITH HAM	TOMATO	1 SOUP CAN MILK 1 SOUP CAN WATER

cooking big

Come one, come all . . . and bring your appetites. Bill of fare: A few good dishes and plenty of each. Here's a batch of crowd-pleasers you can whip together almost effortlessly—18 tasty ways to say, "Come again".

HOMESTYLE CHICKEN SKILLET

4 pounds chicken parts
4 tablespoons shortening
2 cans (11 ounces each)
    condensed Cheddar
    cheese soup
4 teaspoons salt
¼ teaspoon pepper
1 teaspoon poultry
    seasoning

2 cups raw regular rice
2 soup cans water
2 cups chopped canned
    tomatoes
2 packages (9 ounces
    each) frozen Italian
    green beans

Prepare in 2 skillets (10″ each) by dividing ingredients equally. Brown chicken in shortening; pour off fat. Add soup and seasonings. Cover; cook over low heat 15 minutes. Add rice, water, tomatoes, and beans. Bring to boil; stir to separate beans. Reduce heat. Cook covered 30 minutes more or until rice is done. Stir often. Makes 8 servings.

A TIME TO THAW: *When the frost in your freezer gets about ¼ inch thick, defrost. You'll be doing your utility bill a favor since frost makes your freezer work harder to keep the same temperature.*

YANKEE CHILI

1½ pounds ground beef
1 cup chopped onion
2 medium cloves garlic,
    minced
1 can (10½ ounces)
    condensed beef broth
2 cans (10¾ ounces each)
    condensed tomato soup
1 soup can water

2 cans (15½ ounces each)
    kidney beans,
    undrained
3 cups cooked elbow
    macaroni
3 tablespoons chili
    powder
2 tablespoons vinegar

In large saucepan, brown beef and cook onion with garlic until tender (use shortening if necessary). Stir to separate meat. Add remaining ingredients. Simmer 30 minutes; stir occasionally. Makes about 12 cups.

ROMAN CASSEROLE

1 pound ground beef
½ pound hot Italian
   sausage, cut in ½-inch
   slices
1 cup chopped onion
2 teaspoons oregano
   leaves, crushed
1 can (11 ounces)
   condensed Cheddar
   cheese soup

1 can (10¾ ounces)
   condensed tomato soup
1 cup water
4 cups cooked wide
   noodles
4 slices (about 4 ounces)
   Cheddar cheese, cut in
   half diagonally

In skillet, brown beef and cook sausage and onion with oregano until done (use shortening if necessary); stir to separate meat. Pour off fat. Add soups, water, and noodles; pour into 2-quart shallow baking dish (12x8x2"). Cover; bake at 400°F. for 40 minutes or until hot. Uncover; stir. Top with cheese; bake until cheese melts. Makes about 8 cups.

STOVE-TOP MACARONI and CHEESE

1 cup chopped onion
4 tablespoons butter or
   margarine
2 cans (10¾ ounces each)
   condensed cream of
   chicken soup
1½ cups water
1 tablespoon
   Worcestershire
⅛ teaspoon pepper
6 cups cooked elbow
   macaroni
4 cups shredded sharp
   Cheddar cheese (about
   1 pound)
1 package (10 ounces)
   frozen mixed
   vegetables, cooked
   and drained

In large heavy pan, cook onion in butter until tender. Add soup; gradually blend in water. Stir in remaining ingredients. Heat until cheese melts; stir often. Makes about 10½ cups.

HAM 'n' POTATOES HAWAIIAN

1 can (about 8 ounces)
  pineapple slices in
  unsweetened juice
3 cups cooked ham cut in
  strips
6 tablespoons butter or
  margarine
6 cups cubed cooked
  potatoes
1 cup chopped onion
½ cup coarsely chopped
  green pepper

¼ teaspoon thyme leaves,
  crushed
2 cans (10¾ ounces each)
  condensed cream of
  mushroom soup
1 tablespoon
  Worcestershire
⅛ teaspoon pepper
Green pepper rings

Drain pineapple, reserving juice. In large skillet or heavy pan, brown ham in 2 tablespoons butter; remove. In same skillet, brown potatoes and cook onion and chopped green pepper with thyme in 4 tablespoons butter until tender. Stir in ham, soup, reserved juice, Worcestershire, and pepper. Heat; stir occasionally. Garnish with pineapple slices and green pepper rings. Makes about 10 cups.

AU GRATIN FRANKS 'n' POTATOES

6 cups cubed raw
  potatoes
1 cup diced green pepper
1 cup chopped onion
4 tablespoons butter or
  margarine
1 teaspoon salt
¼ teaspoon pepper
1½ pounds frankfurters,
  diagonally sliced

1 can (11 ounces)
  condensed Cheddar
  cheese soup
1 package (3 ounces)
  cream cheese, softened
½ cup water
¼ cup ketchup

In covered large heavy pan, cook potatoes, green pepper, and onion in 3 tablespoons butter until potatoes are *just* tender (about 20 minutes). Stir occasionally. Season with salt and pepper. Push potatoes to the side; add frankfurters and remaining 1 tablespoon butter; brown. In bowl, gradually blend soup into cream cheese until smooth; add water and ketchup. Stir into potato-frankfurter mixture. Heat; stir occasionally. Makes about 9 cups.

OVEN-BARBECUED SPARERIBS

8 pounds spareribs, cut in
  serving-size pieces
2 cans (10½ ounces each)
  condensed onion soup
1 cup chili sauce
¼ cup dry mustard
¼ cup steak sauce

2 tablespoons brown
  sugar
1 tablespoon vinegar
4 teaspoons cornstarch
1 medium clove garlic,
  minced

In large heavy pan, cover spareribs with water. Simmer 1 hour; drain. Arrange in single layer in two 3-quart shallow baking dishes (13 × 9 × 2″). Meanwhile, in saucepan, combine remaining ingredients. Cook over low heat 5 minutes; stir often. Spoon on ribs. Bake at 450°F. for 30 minutes or until done. Makes 8 servings.

SOUPERBURGER

4 pounds ground beef
2 cups chopped onion
2 tablespoons salad oil
4 cans (10¾ ounces each)
  condensed cream of
  mushroom soup

3 tablespoons prepared
  mustard
⅛ teaspoon pepper
Toasted hamburger buns

In large heavy pan, brown beef and cook onion in oil until tender. Stir to separate meat; pour off fat. Stir in soup, mustard, and pepper. Heat; stir occasionally. Serve over buns. Makes about 12 cups.

A KNACK FOR SNACKING: *If your family is dedicated to between-meal munching, make the most of it, nutritionwise. Offer them foods that fit right in with the day's meal plans—fresh fruits and vegetables, hot soups, juices, milk shakes, ice cream, cheese, nuts, oatmeal cookies. In other words, foods that take up where your menu plans leave off to provide servings from the Four Food Groups.*

Meanwhile, banish snacks that offer calories only. You'll be surprised at the savings—with absolutely no sacrifice in nutrients.

NOODLEBURGER SCALLOP

2 pounds ground beef
½ cup chopped celery
2 medium cloves garlic,
   minced
1 teaspoon salt
⅛ teaspoon pepper
1 can (11 ounces)
   condensed Cheddar
   cheese soup

1 can (10¾ ounces)
   condensed cream of
   mushroom soup
⅔ cup milk
½ cup sour cream
4 cups cooked noodles
4 tomato slices, halved
Shredded process cheese

In skillet, brown beef and cook celery with garlic until tender. Pour off fat. Add salt and pepper. In large bowl, blend soups, milk, and sour cream. In two 1½-quart casseroles, layer noodles, meat, and soup mixture. Bake at 400°F. for 25 minutes; stir. Top with tomato and cheese. Bake until cheese melts. Makes 8 servings.

JUMBO TUNA GUMBO

2 cans (10¾ ounces each)
   condensed chicken
   gumbo soup
2 soup cans milk
2 cans (about 7 ounces
   each) tuna, drained and
   flaked

1 can (about 16 ounces)
   cream style corn
2 cups cubed cooked
   potatoes
⅛ teaspoon pepper

In saucepan, combine ingredients. Heat; stir occasionally. Makes about 9½ cups.

IN SEARCH OF THE PERFECT PARTY FOOD ... *easy, economical, enticing. That's cheese. What could be handier than putting together a tray of fruit, bread, crackers, and a variety of cheeses?*

Here's hidden economy, too: No waste. Just refrigerate what is left in airtight containers for future use.

As for enjoyment, you can enhance yours by removing cheese (still covered) from the refrigerator a little while before serving. Almost any cheese, except cream cheese, tastes better this way.

CHICKEN MAJORCA

4 whole chicken breasts
   (about 3 pounds), split
¼ cup shortening
1 can (11 ounces)
   condensed Cheddar
   cheese soup
1 can (10¾ ounces)
   condensed cream of
   chicken soup
1 can (about 4 ounces)
   sliced mushrooms,
   drained
2 tablespoons chopped
   pimiento
½ teaspoon thyme leaves,
   crushed
2 packages (10 ounces
   each) frozen cut
   asparagus

Use 1 large skillet or prepare in 2 skillets (about 10″ each) by dividing ingredients equally. Brown chicken in shortening; pour off fat. Stir in soups, mushrooms, pimiento, and thyme; add asparagus. Cover; cook over low heat 30 minutes or until done. Stir occasionally. Makes 8 servings.

CHICKEN NOODLE SCALLOP

2 cans (10¾ ounces each)
   condensed cream of
   chicken soup
¾ cup sour cream
4 cups cooked noodles
3 cups cubed cooked
   chicken

2 cups cooked peas
1 teaspoon salt
¼ teaspoon pepper
¼ teaspoon rubbed sage

In large heavy pan, blend soup and sour cream. Add remaining ingredients. Heat; stir occasionally. Makes about 10 cups.

Dutch Chowder 'n' Dumplings—recipe page 84

BAKED SPAGHETTI

2 pounds ground beef
½ pound hot Italian
  sausage, sliced
1½ cups chopped onion
2 large cloves garlic,
  minced
1 tablespoon Italian
  seasoning, crushed

4 cans (10¾ ounces each)
  condensed tomato soup
3 soup cans water
1 tablespoon vinegar
2 teaspoons salt
1 pound spaghetti,
  cooked and drained
Grated Parmesan cheese

In large heavy pan, brown beef and cook sausage and onion with garlic and Italian seasoning until done. Stir to separate meat. Stir in soup, water, vinegar, and salt. Simmer 15 minutes; stir occasionally. Add spaghetti. Transfer to two 2½-quart shallow baking dishes (13x9x2″). Bake at 400°F. for 30 minutes or until hot; stir. Top with cheese. Makes about 15 cups.

CANDLELIGHT CHICKEN

1 jar (about 2½ ounces)
  sliced dried beef, rinsed
  and drained
4 whole chicken breasts,
  split, skinned, and
  boned (about 2 pounds
  boneless)
2 cans (10¾ ounces each)
  condensed cream of
  mushroom soup
1 cup sour cream
6 slices bacon, cut in half
Cooked rice

In 2½-quart shallow baking dish (13x9x2″), arrange single layer of beef; top with chicken. Blend soup and sour cream; pour over all. Top with bacon. Bake at 400°F. for 1 hour or until done. Serve with rice. Makes 8 servings.

Autumn Beef Stew—recipe page 90

GOLD RUSH CHICKEN

5 pounds chicken parts
¼ cup melted butter or
   margarine
3 cans (10¾ ounces each)
   condensed golden
   mushroom soup
½ cup sweet vermouth or
   grape juice
½ cup chopped parsley
½ teaspoon poultry
   seasoning

In two 2-quart shallow baking dishes (12x8x2″), arrange
chicken in a single layer skin-side up; brush with butter.
Bake at 400°F. for 45 minutes; baste once with pan drippings. Combine remaining ingredients; spoon over
chicken. Bake 15 minutes more or until done. Makes 10
servings.

SCALLOPED POTATOES PARMESAN

2 cans (11 ounces each)
   condensed Cheddar
   cheese soup
½ cup milk
¼ cup grated Parmesan
   cheese

8 cups thinly sliced
   potatoes
1 cup thinly sliced onion
1 tablespoon butter or
   margarine
Paprika

In bowl, blend soup, milk, and Parmesan. In buttered 3-
quart shallow baking dish (13 × 9 × 2″), arrange alternate
layers of potatoes, onion, and sauce. Dot top with butter;
sprinkle with paprika. Cover; bake at 400°F. for 45 minutes. Uncover; bake 15 minutes more or until potatoes are
tender. Makes about 7½ cups.

DON'T SNUB THE SPUD: *Eat the whole thing. If you eagerly
devour the tender insides of a baked potato—but not the skin—
you're leaving a lot behind. Vitamins are concentrated near the
skin, and the skin itself provides valuable roughage to aid diges-
tion.*

STUFFED TURKEY

6 slices bacon
1 cup sliced celery
½ cup chopped onion
1 package (8½ ounces)
    herb-seasoned stuffing
    mix
2 cups coarse cornbread
    crumbs
1 can (10½ ounces)
    condensed beef broth

1 egg, slightly beaten
10-pound turkey
1 can (10¾ ounces)
    condensed cream of
    mushroom soup
½ cup whole berry
    cranberry sauce
¼ cup orange juice

In skillet, cook bacon until crisp; remove and crumble. Pour off all but 2 tablespoons drippings. Cook celery and onion in drippings until tender. Toss lightly with stuffing mix, cornbread, broth, and egg. Fill cavity of turkey loosely with stuffing. Truss; place in roasting pan. Cover with foil. Roast at 325°F. for about 4 hours (25 minutes per pound or until tender). Uncover last hour to brown. Remove turkey to serving platter. Skim fat from drippings; add remaining ingredients. Heat; stir to loosen browned bits. Makes 12 servings.

SPEEDY TETRAZZINI

1 cup thinly sliced celery
4 tablespoons butter or
    margarine
3 cans (10¾ ounces each)
    condensed Cheddar
    cheese soup

1 can (16 ounces)
    tomatoes, chopped
5 cups cooked spaghetti
3 cans (about 7 ounces
    each) tuna, drained and
    flaked

In large heavy pan, cook celery in butter until tender. Stir in soup. Add remaining ingredients. Heat; stir occasionally. Makes about 9 cups.

et cetera

Appetizers, desserts, vegetables, breads, salads, dressing
sandwiches, beverages—all the little things that mean a lot to you
menus are included in this section. Each is a small treasure guaran
teed to brighten any table, pamper every palate . . . again and again.

CHILI SHRIMP DIP

1 can (10¾ ounces)
  condensed cream of
  shrimp soup
1 package (8 ounces)
  cream cheese, softened

¼ cup finely chopped
  celery
2 tablespoons chili sauce
1 tablespoon finely
  chopped onion
Dash Worcestershire

With electric mixer or rotary beater, gradually blend soup
into cream cheese. Beat *just* until smooth (overbeating
makes dip thin). Stir in remaining ingredients. Chill 4 hours
or more. Serve as a dip with crackers or chips. Makes about
2 cups.

ZIPPY CLAM DIP

1 can (10¾ ounces)
  condensed cream of
  celery soup
1 package (8 ounces)
  cream cheese, softened
1 can (8 ounces) minced
  clams, well-drained

1 tablespoon chopped
  parsley
2 teaspoons prepared
  horseradish

With electric mixer or rotary beater, gradually blend soup
into cream cheese. Beat *just* until smooth (overbeating
makes dip thin). Stir in remaining ingredients. Chill. Serve
as a dip with crackers or chips. Makes about 2½ cups.

CACTUS CORN

4 slices bacon
¼ cup green pepper strips
1 can (11 ounces)
  condensed Cheddar
  cheese soup

3 cups cooked whole
  kernel corn
½ cup drained chopped
  canned tomatoes

In saucepan, cook bacon until crisp; remove and crumble.
Pour off all but 2 tablespoons drippings. Cook green pepper in drippings until tender. Add soup, corn, and tomatoes. Heat; stir occasionally. Garnish with bacon.
Makes about 4 cups.

CARAWAY CHEESE BREAD

6½ to 7 cups sifted
  all-purpose flour
2 packages active dry
  yeast
¼ cup grated Parmesan
  cheese
1 tablespoon caraway
  seed

1 can (11 ounces)
  condensed Cheddar
  cheese soup
1½ cups water
3 tablespoons butter or
  margarine
3 tablespoons sugar
2 teaspoons salt

In large bowl, combine 3 cups flour, yeast, cheese, and caraway. In saucepan, heat remaining ingredients to lukewarm; add to dry ingredients. Beat at low speed of electric mixer 30 seconds, scraping sides of bowl. Beat at high speed 3 minutes. Stir in enough remaining flour to make a stiff dough. Knead until smooth on lightly floured board (about 10 minutes). Place in greased bowl, turning once. Cover; let rise in warm place until doubled (about 1 hour). Punch down. Cover; let rest 10 minutes. Divide dough in half. Shape each half into a loaf. Place each in a greased loaf pan (9x5x3″). Cover; let rise until doubled (about 1 hour). Bake at 400°F. for 30 minutes or until done. Makes 2 loaves.

JACK FROST BEAN BAKE

4 slices bacon
1 cup sliced onion
1 can (10¾ ounces)
  condensed cream of
  mushroom soup
¼ cup chili sauce
1 teaspoon
  Worcestershire

⅛ teaspoon hot pepper
  sauce
2 packages (10 ounces
  each) frozen lima
  beans, cooked and
  drained
½ cup shredded Cheddar
  cheese

In saucepan, cook bacon until crisp; remove and crumble. Pour off all but 2 tablespoons drippings. Cook onion in drippings until tender. Stir in soup, chili sauce, Worcestershire, and hot pepper sauce. Add beans and bacon. Pour into 1½-quart casserole. Bake at 400°F. for 25 minutes or until hot; stir. Top with cheese; bake until cheese melts. Makes about 5 cups.

DANISH PASTRIES

2 packages (14 to 18
ounces each) hot roll
mix
1 can (11 ounces)
condensed Cheddar
cheese soup

2 eggs, slightly beaten
½ cup sugar
½ teaspoon almond
extract

In large bowl, dissolve yeast from both boxes of mix as directed using *only* ¾ cup water. Follow mix directions adding *undiluted* soup, eggs, sugar, and extract with flour mixture. Let rise as directed. Shape dough into 48 small balls; flatten to form 1½-inch circles. Place on lightly greased cookie sheets; let rise again until doubled. Press center of each circle to make indentation; spoon about 1 tablespoon filling* in each. Bake at 375°F. for 20 minutes or until brown. Cool; glaze if desired. Makes 48 pastries.

Fillings: Assorted prepared fruit pie fillings or pineapple cream cheese.

To Make Ahead: Freeze baked pastries in single layer; wrap in freezer wrap.

MEXICALI TACOS

2 pounds ground beef
½ cup chopped green
pepper
1 can (11¼ ounces)
condensed chili beef
soup
1 can (10¾ ounces)
condensed tomato soup

1 to 2 tablespoons finely
chopped cherry
peppers
24 taco shells
Shredded Cheddar or
Monterey Jack cheese
Shredded lettuce
Chopped onion
Diced tomato

In skillet, brown beef and cook green pepper until tender; stir to separate meat. Add soups and cherry peppers. Cook over low heat 5 minutes; stir occasionally. Fill each taco shell with 3 to 4 tablespoons meat mixture; top each with remaining ingredients. Makes 24 tacos.

CHEESECAKE PIE

Crumb Crust:
2 cups fine vanilla wafer or graham cracker crumbs

6 tablespoons butter or margarine, melted
¼ cup sugar

Filling:
12 ounces cream cheese, softened
⅔ cup sugar
3 eggs
1 can (11 ounces) condensed Cheddar cheese soup

2 tablespoons lemon juice
1 teaspoon grated lemon rind
1 teaspoon vanilla extract
¼ teaspoon almond extract

Topping:
1 cup sour cream
¼ cup sugar

1 teaspoon grated lemon rind
1 teaspoon vanilla extract

Crust: Combine crumbs, butter, and sugar. Press firmly into 10″ pie plate. Chill.

Filling: With electric mixer, beat cream cheese until smooth. Add sugar and eggs alternately. Blend in *1 cup* soup, lemon juice, rind, and flavorings. Pour into chilled pie crust. Bake at 350°F. for 50 minutes.

Topping: Blend sour cream, remaining soup, sugar, lemon rind, and vanilla. Spread on pie. Bake 5 minutes more. Cool; chill. Top with prepared fruit pie filling.

THERE'S MORE TO DESSERT THAN A HAPPY SWEET TOOTH:
Stop thinking of dessert as a mere frill. Instead, make it an integral part of every meal plan and reap more nutrition for your money.

Has the day been low in fruits and vegetables? Baked apple dessert to the rescue. Need another serving of milk to round out the family's intake? Let them eat custard for the grand finale. You get the idea—and that sweet tooth needn't suffer a bit.

SEAFOOD DRESSING

1 can (10¾ ounces)
  condensed cream of
  shrimp soup
1 cup mayonnaise
2 chopped hard-cooked
  eggs

¼ cup chili sauce
¼ cup chopped green
  pepper
2 tablespoons finely
  chopped onion
1 teaspoon lemon juice

In bowl, combine ingredients. Serve over crisp salad greens or seafood. Makes about 3 cups.

DILL-SPIKED ONION ROLLS

2 packages (14 to 18
  ounces each) hot roll
  mix
1 can (10¾ ounces)
  condensed cream of
  onion soup

2 eggs, slightly beaten
½ cup grated Parmesan
  cheese
1 tablespoon dried dill
  weed

In large bowl, dissolve yeast from both boxes of mix as directed using *only* ¾ cup water. Follow mix directions adding *undiluted* soup, eggs, cheese, and dill with flour mixture. Let rise as directed. Shape dough into 16 large or 32 small rolls. Place on lightly greased cookie sheets; let rise again until doubled. Bake at 375°F. for 20 minutes or until brown. Makes 16 large or 32 small rolls.

PLAY IT AGAIN, CHEF: *Leftover vegetables? Don't send last night's green beans, carrots, peas, cauliflower, broccoli to Never-Never Land. Add them to tonight's salad greens for a peppy change. Top with grated Parmesan cheese, onion rings, or croutons.*

Leftover meat or poultry? Team them with a little cheese and sliced hard-cooked eggs, to transform ordinary salad greens into a luscious main dish Chef's Salad.

TWICE-BAKED POTATOES

8 medium baking
potatoes
2 tablespoons butter or
margarine
¼ teaspoon salt
1 can (11 ounces)
condensed Cheddar
cheese soup

1 tablespoon chopped
dried chives
Paprika

Bake potatoes until done. Cut potatoes in half lengthwise;
scoop out insides leaving a thin shell. With electric mixer,
mash potatoes with butter and salt. Gradually add soup
and chives; beat until light and fluffy. Spoon into shells.
Sprinkle with paprika. Bake in 2½-quart shallow baking
dish (13x9x2") at 450°F. for 15 minutes or until hot. Makes 8
servings.

SOUTH-of-the-BORDER DIP

1 can (11 ounces)
condensed black bean
soup
1 package (3 ounces)
cream cheese, softened
⅓ cup chopped canned
tomatoes

¼ cup finely chopped
onion
1 tablespoon chopped hot
cherry peppers
2 teaspoons chili powder

With electric mixer or rotary beater, gradually blend soup
into cream cheese. Beat *just* until smooth (overbeating
makes dip thin). Stir in remaining ingredients. Chill 4 hours
or more. Serve as a dip with crackers or chips. Makes about
2 cups.

OPERATION CORNUCOPIA: *Fresh fruits and vegetables are most
plentiful—and priced attractively—in season. That's when to
enjoy them for all they're worth.*

APPLE CRISP

1 can (11 ounces) condensed Cheddar cheese soup
1 cup packed brown sugar
1 teaspoon lemon juice
1 teaspoon ground cinnamon
½ teaspoon ground nutmeg

8 cups very thinly sliced apples (about 8 apples)
¾ cup quick-cooking oats, uncooked
¼ cup chopped walnuts
2 tablespoons milk
1 tablespoon butter or margarine, softened

Combine soup, ¼ cup sugar, lemon juice, cinnamon, and nutmeg. Toss apples with soup mixture; pour into buttered 9″ square or 10″ round baking dish. Combine ¾ cup sugar with remaining ingredients; sprinkle over apples. Bake at 375°F. for 45 minutes or until apples are tender. Allow to stand 15 minutes or more before serving. Serve with a whipped topping or ice cream if desired. Makes about 5½ cups.

CHEESE DIVAN

2 packages (10 ounces each) frozen broccoli spears, cooked and drained
1 can (11 ounces) condensed Cheddar cheese soup

¼ cup sour cream
2 tablespoons milk
1 can (about 8 ounces) whole kernel corn, drained
¼ teaspoon curry powder

In 1½-quart shallow baking dish (10x6x2″), arrange broccoli. Blend soup, sour cream, milk, corn, and curry; pour over broccoli. Bake at 400°F. for 20 minutes or until hot. Garnish with pimiento if desired. Makes 4 to 6 servings.

DON'T THROW IT TO THE BIRDS: *Instead, dry stale bread slices in a slow oven. Crush for bread crumbs. Cube before drying for croutons to pep up soups and salads.*

CHEESY SCALLOPED POTATOES

1 can (10¾ ounces)
  condensed cream of
  mushroom or celery
  soup
½ cup milk
Dash pepper
4 cups thinly sliced
  potatoes

½ cup thinly sliced onion
1 cup shredded sharp
  Cheddar cheese
1 tablespoon butter or
  margarine
Dash paprika

Blend soup, milk, and pepper. In 1½-quart casserole, arrange alternate layers of potatoes, onion, sauce, and cheese. Dot top with butter; sprinkle with paprika. Cover; bake at 375°F. for 1 hour. Uncover; bake 15 minutes more or until done. Makes about 4 cups.

WHICH CUPBOARD, MOTHER HUBBARD? *There are some kitchen cabinets that **should** be bare—of food anyway. Those over the range, near the dishwasher, or by the refrigerator exhaust are too warm for food. Store dishes or pans in these places and save the cooler spots for canned goods and staples to insure longer shelf life.*

TOMATO FRENCH DRESSING

1 can (10¾ ounces)
  condensed tomato soup
½ cup salad oil
¼ cup vinegar
2 tablespoons sugar

1 tablespoon finely
  chopped onion
2 teaspoons dry mustard
1 teaspoon salt
¼ teaspoon pepper

In covered jar or shaker, combine ingredients; chill. Shake well before using. Serve on crisp salad greens. Makes about 2 cups.

DUAL CHEESE LOGS
(Basic Mixture)

**1 can (11½ ounces)
condensed bean with
bacon soup**

**4 cups (1 pound) shredded
sharp Cheddar cheese
½ cup finely chopped
onion**

In large bowl of electric mixer, beat ingredients until *smooth*. Divide mixture in half.

Spicy Nut Log:
Stir into ½ of basic mixture:

**1 tablespoon
Worcestershire
1 small clove garlic,
minced
¼ teaspoon hot pepper
sauce**

Chill. On waxed paper, shape mixture into log (8x1½″); roll in chopped walnuts. Refrigerate.

Taco Cheese Log:
Stir into ½ of basic mixture:

¼ cup taco sauce

Proceed as above for shaping log. Roll in chopped parsley. Refrigerate.

Serve as a spread for breads or crackers. Makes 2 logs.

RHAPSODY IN GREEN: *Salads—cool, crisp, carefree—have saved many a meal from the clutches of monotony. Yet salads themselves can become cliches when the same greens are used over and over.*

Climb out of that iceberg lettuce rut. Brighten your table with romaine, escarole, endive, chicory, watercress, raw spinach, celery tops. The darker the greens, the higher the vitamin and mineral content—and the more nutrition for your money.

Wash greens thoroughly, drain well, roll in paper towels, crisp in refrigerator. In the interest of freshness, make salads at the very last minute. Drooping greens? Perk them up in ice water.

STEAMED PUDDING

2½ cups sifted
  all-purpose flour
1 tablespoon baking
  powder
½ teaspoon baking soda
1 teaspoon ground
  cinnamon
½ teaspoon ground
  nutmeg

2 cups chopped dates
¼ cup shortening
1 cup sugar
1 egg
1 can (10¾ ounces)
  condensed tomato soup

Sift flour with baking powder, soda, and spices; dust dates with small amount of flour mixture. In bowl, cream shortening and sugar; add egg and mix well. Add dry ingredients alternately with soup; stir well after each addition. Fold in dates. Pour into greased 2-quart mold; cover securely with foil. Place on trivet in large pan. Add boiling water to one-half height of mold. Cover; steam 3 hours. Remove mold from water; uncover and loosen edges of pudding with knife. Unmold while hot. Makes 12 servings.

TRATTORIA GREEN BEANS

4 slices bacon
1 cup sliced onion
2 medium cloves garlic,
  minced
1 teaspoon oregano
  leaves, crushed
¼ teaspoon basil leaves,
  crushed

1 can (10¾ ounces)
  condensed tomato soup
¼ cup water
2 packages (9 ounces
  each) frozen cut green
  beans
Grated Parmesan cheese

In skillet, cook bacon until crisp; remove and crumble. Pour off all but 2 tablespoons drippings. Cook onion with garlic, oregano, and basil in drippings until tender. Add soup, water, and beans. Cover; cook over low heat 20 minutes or until beans are tender. Stir occasionally. Garnish with bacon and cheese. Makes about 3½ cups.

APPLESAUCE OATMEAL COOKIES

2 cups all-purpose flour
1½ teaspoons baking
  powder
½ teaspoon baking soda
2 teaspoons ground
  allspice
1 teaspoon ground
  cinnamon
⅛ teaspoon ground
  cloves

1 can (11 ounces)
  condensed Cheddar
  cheese soup
1½ cups packed brown
  sugar
1 cup applesauce
1 cup shortening
2 eggs
2 cups quick-cooking
  oats, uncooked
1 cup seedless raisins
1 cup chopped walnuts

Sift flour, baking powder, baking soda, and spices into large bowl. Add soup, sugar, applesauce, shortening, and eggs. Using electric mixer, beat at medium speed for 2 minutes (300 strokes with spoon), scraping sides and bottom of bowl constantly. Stir in oats, raisins, and nuts. Drop rounded teaspoonfuls on ungreased cookie sheet. Bake at 350°F. for 15 minutes or until lightly browned. Makes about 7½ dozen cookies.

GREEN BEAN BAKE

1 can (10¾ ounces)
  condensed cream of
  mushroom soup
½ cup milk
1 teaspoon soy sauce
Dash pepper

2 packages (9 ounces
  each) frozen green
  beans, cooked and
  drained
1 can (3½ ounces) French
  fried onions

In 1½-quart casserole, combine soup, milk, soy, and pepper; stir in green beans and ½ can onions. Bake at 350°F. for 30 minutes or until hot; stir. Top with remaining onions. Bake 5 minutes more. Makes about 4 cups.

HELP WIPE OUT CELERY SLUMP: *Revive limp celery by placing it in a deep container of water in the refrigerator.*

TOMATO SPICE CAKE MIX

1 package (2 layer) spice
  cake mix
1 can (10¾ ounces)
  condensed tomato soup

½ cup water
2 eggs

Mix *only* above ingredients; following directions on package. If desired, fold in 1 cup chopped walnuts. Bake as directed. Frost with your favorite white frosting.

FRUIT CAKE: After mixing, fold in 1 cup chopped candied fruit and 1 cup chopped walnuts. Bake as directed on package adding about 5 minutes more.

MR. MAC GREGOR'S GARDEN: *Vegetables aren't just for rabbits, you know. When prepared with care and served with flair, they're food for the gods at prices most mortals can afford.*
   *Some friendly advice: Help stamp out overcook. Serve vegetables when **just tender.** Cook in a small amount of water for the shortest time possible. You'll be saving energy as well as flavor, texture, and nutrients.*

ESPAGNOLE SAUCE

1 slice bacon
⅓ cup chopped onion
1 small bay leaf
⅛ teaspoon thyme leaves,
  crushed

1 can (10¾ ounces)
  condensed golden
  mushroom soup
⅓ cup tomato juice
⅓ cup water

In saucepan, cook bacon until crisp; remove and crumble. Cook onion with bay and thyme in drippings until tender. Stir in remaining ingredients. Heat; stir occasionally. Serve over cooked meats, poultry, or vegetables. Makes about 2 cups.

WHAT THE WELL-DRESSED FOOD ITEM WEARS TO THE FREEZER: *Moisture/vapor-proof materials are a must—aluminum foil, polyethylene bags and wraps, freezer film wraps, plastic and metal containers.*

Why is it so important to keep air and moisture out? Because they cause freezer burn which robs food of flavor and eye appeal.

Seal all packages tightly, too. Air seeps in through even the tiniest openings.

What about the shrink-film wrap on meats in self-serve counters? It breathes so it is unsuitable for freezer storage beyond 2 weeks. Overwrap these packages with one of the moisture/vapor-proof materials.

PILAF

½ cup fine noodles,
  broken in pieces
2 tablespoons butter or
  margarine

1 can (10¾ ounces)
  condensed chicken
  broth
⅓ cup water
½ cup raw regular rice

In saucepan, brown noodles in butter; stir often. Add remaining ingredients. Bring to a boil; reduce heat. Cover; cook over low heat 20 minutes or until liquid is absorbed. Stir occasionally. Makes about 2 cups.

MORNAY SAUCE

1 can (10¾ ounces)
  condensed cream of
  mushroom soup
½ cup shredded natural
  Swiss cheese

⅓ cup light cream or milk
2 tablespoons grated
  Parmesan cheese

In saucepan, combine ingredients. Heat until cheese melts; stir often. Serve over cooked meats, poultry, fish, vegetables, or poached eggs. Makes about 1½ cups.

TOMATO SOUP CAKE

2¼ cups cake flour or 2
cups all-purpose flour
1⅓ cups sugar
4 teaspoons baking
powder
1 teaspoon baking soda
1½ teaspoons allspice
1 teaspoon cinnamon

½ teaspoon ground
cloves
1 can (10¾ ounces)
condensed tomato soup
½ cup hydrogenated
shortening
2 eggs
¼ cup water

Preheat oven to 350°F. Generously grease and flour two round layer pans, 8 or 9" or an oblong pan, (13x9x2"). Measure dry ingredients into large bowl. Add soup and shortening. Beat at low to medium speed for 2 minutes (300 strokes with a spoon) scraping sides and bottom of bowl constantly. Add eggs and water. Beat 2 minutes more, scraping bowl frequently. Pour into pans. Bake 35 to 40 minutes. Let stand in pans 10 minutes; remove and cool on rack. Frost with your favorite white frosting. For a 9" tube pan, bake 1 hour.

Nut or Raisin: After mixing, fold in 1 cup chopped nuts or 1 cup raisins. Bake 35 to 40 minutes.

Date and Nut: After mixing, fold in 1 cup chopped walnuts and 1 cup chopped dates. (Use 1 to 2 tablespoons flour to sprinkle over dates while chopping them.) Bake in 9" layers or 13x9x2" pan for 40 to 45 minutes.

ALL 'ROUND BARBECUE SAUCE

1 can (10¾ ounces)
condensed tomato soup
2 to 4 tablespoons sweet
pickle relish
¼ cup finely chopped
onion

1 tablespoon brown sugar
1 tablespoon vinegar
1 tablespoon
Worcestershire

In saucepan, combine ingredients. Cover; cook over low heat 10 minutes. Stir occasionally. Use as a barbecue sauce for chicken, frankfurters, hamburgers, or steak. Makes about 1½ cups.

MINI-PIZZAS

1 can (11 ounces)
  condensed tomato
  bisque soup
1 small clove garlic,
  minced
1 teaspoon oregano
  leaves, crushed
4 English muffins or
  hamburger buns, split
  and toasted
1 cup shredded
  Mozzarella cheese

In saucepan, combine soup, garlic, and oregano. Heat; stir occasionally. Spread soup mixture on muffins; top with cheese. Broil 4 inches from heat until cheese melts. Makes 8 mini-pizzas.

BEEFY BITE-SIZE NIBBLERS

1 pound ground beef
¼ cup finely chopped
  celery
¼ cup finely chopped
  onion
1 can (10¾ ounces)
  condensed cream of
  mushroom soup
2 tablespoons prepared
  barbecue sauce

2 packages (about 8
  ounces each)
  refrigerated crescent
  dinner rolls
¼ cup sour cream
1 tablespoon prepared
  mustard
1 teaspoon prepared
  horseradish

To make filling, in skillet, brown beef and cook celery and onion until tender (use shortening if necessary); stir to separate meat. Pour off fat. Stir in ¼ cup soup and barbecue sauce. Meanwhile, to make roll-ups, on lightly floured board, roll each package of rolls into a 12-inch square. Cut each square into 16 pieces (3 × 3"). Place about 1 tablespoon filling on each square. Roll up; seal ends. Bake at 450°F. for 8 minutes or until brown. Meanwhile, in saucepan, combine remaining soup, sour cream, mustard, and horseradish. Heat a few minutes to blend flavors. Serve as dip with roll-ups. Makes 32 appetizers.

GAZPACHO

1 can (10¾ ounces)
  condensed tomato soup
1 cup water
1 tablespoon olive oil
2 tablespoons wine
  vinegar

1 large clove garlic,
  minced
1 cup chopped cucumber
½ cup chopped green
  pepper
¼ cup chopped onion

Combine soup, water, oil, vinegar, and garlic. Chill 4 hours or more. Serve in chilled bowls. Pass chilled vegetables for garnish. Makes about 2 cups.

Blender Version: Reduce to ½ cup chopped cucumber, ¼ cup chopped green pepper, and 2 tablespoons chopped onion. In blender, combine all ingredients and 1 slice toast. Blend until smooth. Chill 4 hours or more. Serve in chilled bowls. Pass additional chilled vegetables for garnish. Makes about 3 cups.

MARINATED VEGETABLE SALAD

1 can (10¾ ounces)
  condensed chicken
  broth
4 medium carrots (about
  ½ pound), sliced
2 cups cauliflowerets
2 small zucchini (about
  ½ pound), diagonally
  sliced

1 cup (about ¼ pound)
  sliced mushrooms
¼ cup wine vinegar
1 envelope (about 0.6
  ounce) Italian
  dressing mix

In saucepan, bring broth to boil. Add carrots; simmer 2 minutes. Cool. Stir in remaining ingredients. Chill 4 hours or more. Makes about 7 cups.

COLD CASH: If you have adequate freezer space, buy perishable specials in large quantities and use when needed. Be sure to rotate your stock, using the oldest items first.

CHEAPER BY THE OVENFUL: To get the most cooking done for your money, use your oven to capacity whenever you turn it on. Plan several oven dishes for one meal—baked potatoes and muffins with a casserole, for instance.

SPREAD-a-BURGER

1 can (10¾ ounces)
  condensed tomato soup
1 tablespoon prepared
  mustard
1 tablespoon
  Worcestershire
1 teaspoon prepared
  horseradish
1½ pounds ground beef

⅓ cup finely chopped
  onion
1 teaspoon salt
Generous dash pepper
6 long hard rolls or
  frankfurter buns, slit
  and lightly toasted
Sliced process cheese

Combine soup, mustard, Worcestershire, and horseradish. Mix *thoroughly* ⅓ cup soup mixture, beef, onion, salt, and pepper. Spread evenly on buns; *cover edges completely.* Bake at 400°F. for 10 minutes. Top with remaining soup mixture and cheese; bake 5 minutes more. Makes 6 sandwiches.

GERMAN POTATO SALAD

4 slices bacon
¾ cup chopped onion
1 can (10¾ ounces)
  condensed cream of
  chicken soup
¼ cup water

2 to 3 tablespoons vinegar
½ teaspoon sugar
⅛ teaspoon pepper
4 cups sliced cooked
  potatoes
¼ cup chopped parsley

In skillet, cook bacon until crisp; remove and crumble. Cook onion in drippings until tender. Blend in soup, water, vinegar, sugar, and pepper. Add potatoes, parsley, and bacon. Heat; stir occasionally. Makes about 4 cups.

the meaning of metric

[ruler illustration] 1 INCH

[ruler illustration] 1 CENTIMETER

It's a fact: The National Bureau of Standards has recommended to Congress that it is in the best interest of the United States to adopt the metric system of measurement. Used by most other countries, metric is simpler than our present system. Conversion will be carried out gradually over a 10-year period, giving everyone plenty of time to adjust.

What does this mean to you? First, it means that the food you buy will be marked in grams and kilograms of weight instead of ounces and pounds. Or in liters in place of pints, quarts, and gallons.

1 QUART   ¼ CUP

= 1 LITER
(Approximately)

1 TEASPOON

■ 5 MILLILITERS

■ 15 MILLILITERS

1 TABLESPOON

1 GRAM ■ [spoon illustration]
¼ TEASPOON

KILOGRAM = 1 LB. BUTTER + 1 LB. BUTTER + 6 TABLESPOONS

CELSIUS FAHRENHEIT

100°C. → ← 212°F. Water Boils*

* At sea level.

1 cup — 250 milliliters
¾ cup — 200 milliliters
— 150 milliliters
½ cup — 100 milliliters
¼ cup — 50 milliliters

20°C. → ← 68°F. Room Temperature

0°C. → ← 32°F. Water Freezes

Kitchen measuring utensils will give readings in liters and milliliters rather than teaspoons, tablespoons, cups, pints, quarts, and gallons.

Baking pans will be sized in centimeters instead of inches. Oven, refrigerator, and freezer temperatures will measure Degrees Celsius in place of Degrees Fahrenheit.

Eventually, new recipes will be published which reflect these changes. What will happen to your old favorite recipes? You'll keep on making them the tried and true way, since there's room in every kitchen for two sets of measurers.

everyday equivalents

Apples . . . . 1 lb. . . . . 3 medium (3 cups sliced)

Bananas . . . . 1 lb. . . . . 3 medium (2½ cups sliced)

Berries . . . . 1 pt. . . . . 1¾ cups

Bread . . . . 1 lb. loaf . . . . 14 to 20 slices

Bread Crumbs . . . . . . 1 slice bread, ... ⅓ cup crumbs or

                       dry or soft . . . . ¾ cup cubes

Butter . . . . 1 stick . . . . 4 oz. or 8 tbsp. or ½ cup

Cheese, Cheddar . . . . ¼ lb. . . . . 1 cup shredded

Cream, Heavy . . . . . . ½ pt. . . . . 1 cup (2 cups whipped)

Flour, All-purpose . . . 1 lb. . . . . 4 cups, sifted

   Cake . . . . 1 lb. . . . . 4½ cups, sifted

Lemon . . . . 1 medium . . . . 3 tbsp. juice

                       1 tbsp. grated peel

Macaroni . . . . 1 cup uncooked . . . 2 to 2¼ cups cooked

             ½ lb. uncooked . . . 4 cups cooked

Noodles . . . . 1 cup uncooked . . . 1¾ cups cooked

             ½ lb. uncooked . . . 4 to 5 cups cooked

Onion . . . . 1 small . . . . ¼ cup chopped

             1 medium . . . . ½ cup chopped

             1 large . . . . 1 cup chopped

Orange . . . . 1 medium . . . . ⅓ to ½ cup juice

                       2 tbsp. grated peel

Potatoes, White . . . . 1 lb. . . . . 3 medium

                       2⅓ to 2½ cups sliced

                       2 cups mashed

   Sweet . . . . 1 lb. . . . . 3 medium

                       2½ to 3 cups sliced

Rice, Regular . . . . . . 1 lb. . . . . 2½ cups uncooked

                       8 cups cooked

Sugar, Granulated . . . 1 lb. . . . . 2¼ to 2½ cups

   Brown . . . . 1 lb. . . . . 2¼ cups packed

   Confectioners' . . . . 1 lb. . . . . 4 to 4½ cups unsifted

                       4½ to 5 cups sifted

Tomatoes . . . . 1 lb. . . . . 3 medium

in-a-pinch substitutions

1 tablespoon cornstarch . . . . . . 2 tablespoons flour (approximately)
   (for thickening)

1 cup fresh whole milk . . . . . . ½ cup evaporated milk plus ½ cup water
                                           OR
                                     1 cup reconstituted nonfat dry milk plus
                                     2 tablespoons butter

1 cup sour milk or buttermilk . . 1 tablespoon lemon juice or vinegar plus
                                     enough whole milk to make 1 cup

1 square unsweetened . . . . 3 tablespoons cocoa plus 1 tablespoon fat
   chocolate (1 oz.)

1 cup honey . . . . 1¼ cups sugar plus ¼ cup liquid

1 tablespoon fresh herbs . . . . . 1 teaspoon crumbled dry herbs

1 pound fresh mushrooms . . . . . 6 ounces canned

1 cup canned tomatoes . . . . . . approximately 1⅓ cups cut-up fresh
                                     tomatoes, simmered 10 minutes

this = that

1 gallon = 4 quarts	= 8 pints	= 16 cups	= 128 ounces or 8 pounds
1 quart	= 2 pints	= 4 cups	= 32 ounces or 2 pounds
1 pint	= 2 cups	= 16 ounces or 1 pound
1 cup	= 8 ounces or ½ pound

☆   ☆   ☆   ☆   ☆

1 cup = 16 tablespoons
½ cup = 8 tablespoons
⅓ cup = 5 tablespoons + 1 teaspoon
¼ cup = 4 tablespoons
⅛ cup = 2 tablespoons

☆   ☆   ☆   ☆   ☆

2 tablespoons = 1 ounce
1 tablespoon = 3 teaspoons

household hints

WHAT A DIFFERENCE A DAY MAKES: — *in the price of bread, at any rate. Watch for day-old specials and stock up the freezer.*

THE BIGGER THE CHEAPER, USUALLY: *Food in large containers generally costs less per ounce, pound, or pint than the same thing in smaller packages. But bigger is better only IF you use the contents often or in large quantities.*

A GOOD EGG: *Store eggs unwashed to protect the coating which keeps them fresh.*

DIVIDE AND CONQUER: *By dividing an electric skillet with foil inserts, you can prepare several small dishes at the same time and save electricity to boot.*

JACK FROST IN VEGETABLE LAND: *Large bags of frozen vegetables usually cost less per ounce than small-sized packages. Pour out just the amount you need and return the rest to the freezer.*

THE TELLTALE TOTAL: *Take along a purse-sized adder to total your purchases as you select them at the market. If the total nears your spending limit, check the foods on your list—as well as those already in the shopping cart—to see what unnecessary items you can omit.*

HOW SWEET IT IS: *There are many tasty uses for the syrup that you drain from canned or frozen fruits. Here are four:*
- *When making gelatin salads or desserts, replace part of the water with syrup.*
- *Combine syrup with mayonnaise, and presto—the perfect dressing for fruit salad.*
- *Thicken syrup with cornstarch for meat glazes or dessert sauces.*
- *Flavor milk or fruit drinks with syrup.*

THE NOTHING-A-DAY POLICY OF CONTAINMENT: *Hold on to those reusable containers (with lids) and use them to store everything from mushrooms to minestrone in refrigerator or freezer. Saves a bundle on throw-away wrapping material.*

WHICH CUPBOARD, MOTHER HUBBARD? *There are some kitchen cabinets that should be bare—of food anyway. Those over the range, near the dishwasher, or by the refrigerator exhaust are too warm for food. Store dishes or pans in these places and save the cooler spots for canned goods and staples to insure longer shelf life.*

LOOK FOR THE SILVER LINING: *But not in your oven. Aluminum foil-lined ovens are less efficient, more costly to operate.*

HOW LOW CAN YOU GO? *Try 25°F. That's the amount to lower your oven setting every time you use glass or ceramic utensils, since these materials transfer heat better than metal.*

JUST AN OLD SOFTY: *To keep brown sugar soft, put it in a plastic bag or a jar with a tight lid, and slip in an apple slice for good measure. Check every so often to see that the slice has not dried out.*

SWEET SOMETHINGS: *If you like the taste of sweet potatoes, do not refrigerate. Temperatures below 50°F. cause starch changes which alter the flavor. This high-in-vitamin A vegetable keeps best in a cool, dark place.*

I'D RATHER CUT IT MYSELF! *Whole chickens are usually cheaper than chicken parts, so being your own butcher is just a matter of common cents. For an even bigger budget bonus, buy several whole chickens at sale time, cut them up, then freeze packages of breasts, legs, etc. for up to 10 months.*

PARSLEY, SAGE, ROSEMARY, AND THYME: *There is nothing like an herb—or a subtle combination of them—to take an everyday dish out of this world for practically nothing. Become familiar with herbs. Buy them dried or fresh, or better yet, grow your own.*
   Fresh herbs do boast the best flavor, but caution—they are usually stronger.

index

133

Cactus Corn—recipe page 107
Tomato French Dressing—recipe page 114
Mexicali Tacos—recipe page 109

Cheesecake Pie—recipe page 110
Dill-Spiked Onion Rolls—recipe page 111
Chili Shrimp Dip—recipe page 107

notes

notes

notes

notes